Tracing Journey of India's Defence Budget and Its Future

An analysis

Soumya Awasthi

Department of Defence and Strategic Studies
Savitribai Puhle University of Pune, Pune

GAURAV Book Centre
Private Limited

Publisher
GAURAV BOOK CENTRE PVT LTD
4832/24,Prahlad Lane,S-207 Ansari
Road, Daryaganj, Delhi-110002
Ph.: 43570976, 23278261
Email: gauravbookcentre@gmail.com

Edition: 2015

ISBN: 978-93-83316-24-3

Laser Typesetting
JEE-VEE Graphics # 09911902109

Price: 925/-

Printed
Vikas Computers, Delhi

Dedicated to
In The Loving Memory of
My Nana - Nani
&
Dadi - Baba

Preface

Defence Expenditure constitutes an important part of the Government expenditure and needs detailed economic analysis. There are not many detailed studies analysing defence expenditure in India from the economic point of view. The economic issues have gained relative supremacy over all the other issues in the recent past, especially after the end of the allocation of expenditure and determinants of defence budget assume greater importance. This is especially true in the case of developing countries, which have to manage development along with stability. In the present study the attempt is made to analyse some of the important issues related to defence expenditure through an empirical economic analysis.

This research study was conducted in Department for Defence and Strategic Studies of Savitribhai Puhle University of Pune during 2012-13.

This study was made possible through the help of several individuals and institutions. Firstly I would like to thank Dr. ShantanaVarma, Dr. Navneeta Chedha Behra and Dr. Achin Vinayak from University of Delhi, for making me understand the whole idea of hard power, soft power and strategic affairs; Brig. (retd) Rumel Dhaiya, DDG, IDSA who encouraged me to take the study in this field; Lt.Gen (retd) Y.S Bammi, Dr. Anit Mukherjee, Dr. Shivendra Singh, Brgd. Mandip Singh, and my office colleague Dr. Amit Kumar. I want to convey my special thanks and a deep sense of gratitude to Dr. Shrikant Paranjpe, my mentor for believing in me and also for always being patient with me. Finally, I know all my friends will be looking for their names. My special thanks go to my husband Maj. Sushant Awasthi for extending all the support and believing in me, my mother, father, in-laws, siblings, also my friends Capt. Viabhav Srivastava, Maj. Gaurav Bhatia from College of Military Engineering, Pune. My dear friend Naresh Gupta, Shruti Khurana, Bikanshu Singh, Radu Nicholas Botez Akash S. Gaud, friends from University of Pune Aditi Puranik, Sameer Mallaya, and the staff of the Department of Defence and Strategic Studies.

Soumya Awasthi

Contents

List of Tables

Appendix

Chapter 1

Introduction

Two of the unwavering realities of international politics are the primacy of national self interest and the importance of military power as a factor in international relations. No government however pacific minded has ever been able to rely solely upon the political ethics of other stated or upon its own diplomacy to deter direct attack or interference with its external interests. Armies have, therefore been a feature of every state in recorded history.

Total security has rarely been possible even for the most powerful of nations, and the basic dilemma of defence policy- how to achieve maximum security with minimum expenditure on the armed forces- has never allowed of a simple solution. Every contingency cannot be provided for, and strategy, like politics- to which it is closely bound- is always a choice between alternatives. A nation's quest for security can never be conducted heedless of the antagonism which that search may provoke among other powers or among its own people. There must always be a considered relationship between commitments and power and between power and resources. There must also be a willingness to employ such forms of power as may be the territorial integrity and political independence of the state. The essence of a sound national security policy is for government to define the nation's vital interests and to develop sufficient power, alone or in concert with others, to secure those interests.

Defence expenditure constitutes an important part of Government expenditure and needs detailed economic analysis. There are not many detailed studies analysing defence expenditure in India from the economic point of view. The economic issues have gained relative supremacy over all the other issues in the recent past, especially after the end of the allocation of expenditure and determinants of defence budget assume greater importance. This is especially true in the case of developing countries, which have to manage development along with stability.

In the present study the attempt is made to analyse some of the important issues related to defence expenditure through an empirical economic analysis.

In this study, the need for redefinition of defence expenditure has been stressed and attempt has been made to incorporate dual purpose technology areas, paramilitary, internal security, and other related supportive expenditures on defence for a more realistic analysis. While doing this, care is taken to account for methodological discrepancies, data constraints and the limitations of statistical techniques.

This study attempts to analyse the following hypotheses:

1. Discuss what is defence budget, how is it formulated and why it is necessary to analyse and study defence budget.
2. A trend analysis of India's defence Budget since 1950 to till date.

   In order to, track the GDP and the CGE in percentage with every financial year.
3. Through analysis of external and internal threats understand the trend of the defence budget particularly after Indo-China War in 1962 and internal threats in 1980s.
4. Analysis of the functioning and the causes of delay in the modernisation and upgradation of Armed Forces.

Defence expenditure is considered as an inevitable expenditure for the survival of a nation state in the world as well as it is necessary to protect the development of a nation from various kinds of threat. However, not many people in the academic community have discussed and analysed this area. Hence an attempt is made here to elaborate the concept of defence expenditure and its various other aspects.

In this study the defence expenditure for the period 1950- 2014, including 1962, 1965, 1971 and 1999 war has been analysed. The focus of the study is on post war period which were the most crucial for India for several reasons.

In the 1962 war India was worst hit by the Chinese intrusion and at the same time there were major problem in the internal politics and environment of the nation. India was both militarily and economically affected in this period.

In the 1971 war India established its military supremacy in South Asia and its marks watershed in Indian history. In the 1971 war India established its military supremacy in South Asia and it marks watershed Indian history. During this period India did not face any external aggression or threat but was facing lot of internal security threats and low intensity conflict which also led to the increase in the defence budget. The role of armed forces was restricted to the border but was involved in internal issues as well.

It is mainly in this period that the Indian planners realised that defence and development are not competitive but complimentary to each other and India tried to enhance its economic capability. Therefore there is an attempt to focus on the role of armed forces, how budget is formulated and the discussion of development versus defence.

For defence expenditure and other supportive expenditure analyses a large number of primary sources pertaining to a number of years have been explored. These include the Union Budget, Demand for Grants of various ministries and Departments, Annual Plans, Five Year Plans of Government of India, Pay Commission reports, Defence Service Estimates, Annual Reports of Ministry of Defence, Reserve Bank of India Archives.

Along with that Defence Procurement Procedure Manual, Defence Doctrine for the understanding of the method and procedure of procurement and modernisation plan.

The present study follows the historical- analytical method. The availability of original sources in the form of government documents and statistical data made it possible to employ this approach. The theoretical and conceptual data is also analysed. The numerical data is used for Statistical analysis.

The data about the defence expenditure of India and other defence related items have been collected from Defence Service Estimates of Government of India, Ministry of Defence.

The Military Balance and SIPRI Year Book for various years and Institute for Defence Studies and Analysis (IDSA) New Delhi Publications have been used for collecting comparative statistical data of defence expenditure.

The data about Gross Domestic Product (GDP) and Comparative Government Expenditure (CGE) have been collected from the Reserve Bank of India's Currency and Finance Report for various years and archives.

The actual total expenditure at current prices of various Ministries/Departments are Gross Expenditures on it and the recoveries and receipts are not adjusted.

The breakup of expenditure is given only of important items and programmes. The expenditure shown in the break ups are Revised Estimates only and they are not actual expenditures.

For analysis of Defence Expenditure macro indicator of Gross Domestic Product has been deployed. And as percent of Central Government Expenditure (CGE) is also given for the comparisons of Defence Expenditure with the rest of the expenditures.

In order to get a clear picture of the defence expenditure, burden, the percentage share of the defence expenditure to total gross expenditure has been presented.

Methodology used for interpretation of data – the tables has been constructed for total expenditure on Army, Navy and Air Force in percentage and current price. Table is also added for the percentage of defence expenditure in terms of GDP and CGE.

The Net Expenditure is shown as a total Defence Expenditure and the Revenue Defence Expenditure is divided into allocations for Army, Navy, Air Force and Ordinance Factory. Similarly the Capital Defence Expenditure account it is divided on Army (Capital), Navy (Capital) and Air Force (Capital).

In some tables figures don't tally because in defence expenditure as per convention many expenditure items remain unclassified. Sometimes totals/percentages don't tally also on account of changes in the basic definition, budgeting methods, accounting methods in Defence Service Estimates. It is also found that defence Service Estimates do not clearly mention changes in the basic definitions of items of expenditure.

Security is one of the most important concerns of a nation state. Security of a nation from external threats and attack was traditional definition of national security. The first definition of national security as given by Walter Lipmann took into account only military dimension.[1] But it is essential to widen the scope in the changing political situations. Hence one needs a broader definition of national security today and it should contain economic, political, diplomatic and social dimension in addition to the military dimension.

K. Subramanyam (1973), A.P Rana (1976), Jayantanija Bandhopadhyaya (1980), Ravi Nanda (1987), P. V Kamath (1990) supported this idea of broadening the definition of national security. Therefore out of many dimensions military dimension is the most important and inevitable part of the government expenditure.

---

1. Bekonwitz M. and Block P.Q., (1968)"National Security", International Encyclopedia of Social Sciences, Vol. XI New York, The Mac Millan Company and Free Press, , p. 39-40

The subject of defence expenditure is not widely analysed and discussed as a result not many studies exists in India.

The present review is not the exhaustive one but the literature related to defence expenditure can be divided on the basis of the above issues as follows:

There are various studies which tried to give strong linkage between economic power and military power. Among these studies economic power is considered as major determinant of military power and military capability of a nation rest on the infrastructure of economic strength. This view is supported by Subramanyam K., Thomas Raju G.C, Brown Herald, Adam Smith, and Loren J Kavic in their work.

Everybody gains from defence and therefore everybody should pay for it. But here Adam Smith favoured the poor and said that they should be exempted from the payments even though they gained from the provision of it.[2]

Karl Marx did not write specifically about economics of defence but his collaborator, Engels analysed this subject. The changes in the technology have revolutionised some aspects of defence economics and this was the area of study for Engels. He tried to build a relationship between technological changes and military tactics.[3]

Lord Keynes resolved this problem by making theoretical contribution that explained the 'paradox of thrift', in his book 'General Theory'.[4]

All the economists from Adam Smith till Keynes held the common view about the non-developmental nature of the defence expenditure. Yet it found that military expenditure continues to rise in an inexorable fashion in the world.

---

2. Kennedy Gavin, (1975), Economics of Defence, London, Faber and Faber, p. 26
3. Kennedy, Gavin, op. cit., p. 33
4. Kennedy, Gavin, op. cit., p. 37

Therefore, everyone accepts that the defence expenditure is unavoidable and is an essential expenditure.

The area of defence budget determination is analysed by some of the researchers and experts. The determinants of defence include a complete set of domestic, regional and global factors which determine military budget of the developing countries and they vary from country to country. Among the economic factors the most important determinant of the defence budget according to them was the share of Central Government budget in GDP.

A similar view is given by Deger and Sen (1988) and in their work they concluded that the military spending in the developing countries depends upon strategic considerations of threat and security. Some of the contributors to this determinant are Thomas Raju (1978), Deger and Sen (1988), Nicole (1981), Pandase (1990), Lakshmi (1988), Jagjit Singh (1987).

There are few studies done in India for the analysis of defence budget determinants. The important one is by Thomas Raju (1978). In this work he threw a light on the factors which decide how much to be allocated for defence in India. According to him it is governed by three essential factors:

1. Indian perception of external and internal threats.
2. Political structure and political decision-making process in India i.e. budgetary process.
3. Economic capacity or economic potential and economic constraints.[5] This work does not take into account internal security threats separately which has been an important determinant. It also did not analyse these threats in depth.

Lakshmi (1988) substantiates the above determinants of defence budget in her study. She stressed the economic capability of a nation and threat perceptions of military and political leaders as

---

5. Thomas Raju G.C.,(1980),Defence of India: A Budgetary Perspective of Strategy and Politics ,Meerut: The McMillan Company of India Ltd. 1978), p. 7

important defence budget determinants of India for the period 1962-1986.[6]

Similar view is expressed by Pandase (1993) in his article[7] and Paranape (1990) in his article also had substantiated the same view and the similar or the same defence expenditure determinants.[8]

Naik (1990) and Paranjape (1991), have added an element of cost of modernisation programme of armed forced and development of emerging technology areas/dual technology purpose area as an additional domestic key factor for deciding defence outlays in the present era through their works. [9]

Before 1947, India was a part of the British Empire and Indian leaders and opinion shapers were no longer concerned about external security decisions. Hence till 1947 Indian did not play any significant role in shaping of the Indian Defence Policy.

India did not join either Eastern or Western Military Alliances and adopted the policy of Non Alignment. It tried to resolve the disputed issues with its neighbours on the basis of peaceful methods. However this type of defence policy based on non-alignment failed in 1962 after the Sino- India war. This shows that there was no in depth defence policy study and proper defence policy making till 1962. This view is supported in the works related to India's defence policy and it include study by Kavic (1967), Khera (1968), Subramanyam (1973), Rao (1976) etc. these scholars have explored the area of defence policy making in India in detail.

Rao held the view that 1962, 1965 and 1971 wars had forced India to understand the importance of in-depth study of defence

---

6. Y. Lakshmi, (1998) 'Trends in India's Defence Expenditure' ,New Delhi, ABC Publishing House, p. 123-127
7. Pandse K.S.,(1993)"India's Defence and Development", Indian Journal of Strategic Studies, Vol. XVIII (Allahabad, University of Allahabad, , P. 21-34
8. Paranjape, H.K., (1999)"How Much defence expenditure can India Afford", Mainstream Vol. XXVIII, No. 28, New Delhi, p. 6-9
9. Naik M.B.,(1999), "The Defence Budget" Janata, Vol45, No. 13, Bombay, p. 13

policy.[10] Rao (1976), Thomas Raju (1986) and Nanda (1991) have highlighted organisational lacunae in Indian defence policy making. Rao feels that the decision- making apparatus had been properly institutionalised in India but it lacks co-ordination.

Kavic, Khera and Rao have concentrated on 1947 to 1965 time period. The others have taken a review of the whole period till 1990s. The work on security policies of developing countries analysed by Thomas Raju (1982) has been categorised in three factors:

1. Prime Minister
2. Part politics and parliamentary debate
3. Influence of public opinion on defence policy making in India.

On the other hand Kavic concluded that military experts (Chief of Staff Committee) influenced the defence policy making in India than non- military parts of institutional structures and were in minority in defence policy making in 1947-1965.[11]

Smith and Nanda have criticised Indian defence policy in 1980s and 1990s. Smith has concluded that India has over extended its modernisation and weapon procurement programmes in 1980s and 1990s due to which since 1988 India is facing serious problems in economic and defence sector. This shows that defence policy did not match with resources.

A continuous rise in defence expenditure of India is well supported in al studies related to it. In these studies internal, external threats perceptions, economic capabilities, need of armed forces are used to justify the resources allocations for defence in India. The notable studies for defence expenditure analysis of India include Thomas Raju (1978), Lakshmi (1988 etc.

---

10. Rao P.V.R,(1976),India's Defence Policy and Organisation Since Independence, USI National Security Lectures, New Delhi: USI-United Service Institution of Indian Publication, p. 6-8
11. Rao P.V.R,(1976),India's Defence Policy and Organisation Since Independence, USI National Security Lectures, New Delhi: USI-United Service Institution of Indian Publication, p. 6-8

Thomas Raju (1978) has analysed Indian defence budget in three phases

(1) 1947-62, (2) 1962-72, (3) 1971-1974[12]

Lakshmi (1988) divided total expenditure period of her study 1962-86 into four phases:

1. War years 1962-63 to 1971-72
2. Post war years 1971-72 to 1978-79
3. Janata Years 1977-79 to 1979-80
4. The return of Indira Gandhi years 1980-89 to 1985-86.

The 1962 and 1971 war was taken as main points for the phases of defence expenditure analysis. The defence expenditure has been continuously rising in India due to changes in security scenario at external and domestic levels since independence.

The changes in institutions, actors and defence policy, modernisation programmes, arms build up of adversaries; changes in the types and nature of threats, changes in economic capability are used as a basis to explain service wise distribution patterns of defence expenditure by Thomas Raju and Lakshmi.

The analysis by Thomas and Lakshmi prove that a very large share of Army allocation were absorbed by Pay, Pensions and followed by the stores.

A review taken by Institute for Defence Studies and Analysis (IDSA), on Trends in India's defence expenditure substantiate the above empirical analysis.

The frequent use of Army in the sensitive areas of internal security is criticised by Jacob[13] and Lakshmi in their works.[14] The role of private sector in defence production and the problems

---

12. Kavic L.(1967), India's Quest for Security: Defence Policies 1947-1965, California, University of California Press, , p. 217.
13. Jacob G., (1985)"India's Army", Asian Defence Journal, No 9, New York, Sept., p.4
14. Thomas Raju G.C.,(1978),Defence of India: A Budgetary Perspective of Strategy and Politics, Meerut, The Mac Millan Company of India, Ltd., p 23

of defence production sector in the area of defence in 1990 is supported and discussed by Kumar (1991), Rajiv (1991), Mahapatra (1993), Singh (1993), Khanna and Mehrotra (1993) through their work.

Chapter 2

What and Why Defence Budget?

A military budget or expenditure, also known as a defence budget, is the amount of financial resources devoted by a nation, to raise and maintain armed forces. Defence budget also indicates how a nation visions the prospect of threats against it, or the level of aggression it aims to project. The size of a budget also reflects the nation's capability to finance military activities.[1]

There is no universally suitable definition of what constitutes defence budget. However numbers of organisations have developed some definitions. The Stockholm International Peace and Research Institute (SIPRI) seek to include in its definition of military expenditure all costs incurred as a result of current military activities. The guideline definition used by SIPRI includes expenditure on the following actors and activities: (a) the armed forces, including peacekeeping forces; (b) defence ministries and other government agencies engaged in defence projects; (c) paramilitary forces, when judged to be trained and equipped for military operations; and (d) military space activities.

It includes all current and capital expenditure on: (a) military and civil personnel, including retirement pensions of military personnel and social services for personnel; (b) operations and maintenance; (c) procurement; (d) military research and development; and (e) military aid (in the military expenditure of the donor country). It does not include civil defence and current

1. Stockholm International Peace research Institute, "Monitoring Military Expenditures", http://www.sipri.org/research/armaments/milex/measuring-military-expenditures (Accessed in March 2013)

expenditure for past military activities, such as for veterans' benefits, demobilization, conversion and weapon destruction.[2]

Apart from SIPRI, the NATO definition includes current and capital expenditure, paramilitary and police, research and development, military aid etc. [3]

These definitions are in many ways similar to each other, the major difference being the inclusion or exclusion of military aid, paramilitary forces etc.

In simple terms Defence Budget means the money spent on the various plans and activities also the money spent on the training and day to day expenses of the defence personnel's, apart from the seasonal or yearly purchase of the cyclic equipments and other materials which withers away with end of their life span.

Requirement of Defence or Defence Budget

According to the theory given by Adam Smith on the defence expenditure, he wrote in1776, "The first duty of any sovereign nation is that of protecting its society, it can be performed only by means of a military force..." thus the answer to the question as to why any nation need an army at first place is described by Adam Smith specially in the modern day when the war is not fought just for glory but is also for the profit and for the vision of the national interests.[4]

Another explanation by Walter Lipmann explicitly defines National security of which the military is the most important ingredient. According to him, 'A nation has a security when it does not have to sacrifice its legitimate interests to avoid war and is able, if challenged, to preserve them by war'.[5] Therefore

---

2. Ibid.
3. Paranjpe Shrikant, (1999) 'A Framework for Analysis of India's Security Expenditures', "Perspectives on India's Defence and Arms Control" ed., University of Mumbai, Department of Civics and Politics.
4. Kennedy Gavin,(1975) 'The Economics of Defence', Faber and Faber, London
5. Athawale. S. Sanhita (2004), "Defence Services", New Delhi, Anmol Publications Pvt. Ltd.

having an army is not only for a group of individuals or opulent but also for the common man and common good of the society and the nation interest.

India has proved to be a key global power, driven by a robust economic growth and a past of longstanding moral leadership on core humanitarian and geopolitical issues. But, in recent past, the emergence of ideology linked terrorism, the spread of small arms and light weapons (SALW) (Somali Pirates etc), the proliferation of Weapons of Mass Destruction (WMD) (including Nuclear weapons) and globalization of its economy are some of the factors which link India's security directly with the extended neighbourhood.

It then becomes imperative for the nation to have a strong defence capabilities, that would help safeguard the economic, cultural and social prosperity generated over last couple of decades and also protect key economic interests like trade routes, safety etc going forward.

Adam Smith was one of the first economists who justified the expenses on defence as the first duty of the government. Defence expenditure ensures national freedom and other advantages. Every nation in the world is determined either by conserving its core values or extending its national goals. There is a possibility that while pursuing these goals other nations are likely to be affected and due to this the threat of war never fading from the world. Because of this danger of escalation of war and a threat to the territorial integrity, sovereignty, and survival, all the countries of the world are spending large amount of money and resources on their national defence. [6]

With the military expenses comes the national security and sovereignty, which in turn ensures the success in the execution of foreign policy goals and maintenance of national security against both external and internal threats. Therefore, defence

---

6. Kennedy Gavin,(1975) 'The Economics of Defence', Faber and Faber, London

spending has become essential and inevitable part of any nation's economy.

In fact, Kautilya in his book Arthshastra mentions about the interdependence of military and economic power where he explains 'a country's military capability is derived from its economic capacity.[7] A country's economic capacity also determines its capability to exert and preserve its political, social and economic independence in the world and hence a force. Economic power does not translate directly into military power but the material basis of military strength has traditionally been a foundation for assessments of military potential, and economic capacity has been treated as a necessary condition for the ability to inflict significant harm since the advent of industrial age.

In short, civil military relations are effectively employed in the economic development of a country. Defence spending provides security to the life and property of the people. It also ensures trade and prosperity of the nation. Military power helps the nation in projecting it as a powerful entity in domestic and external environment.

Several economists and war analysts have given their own suggestions on what kind of army a nation can have and how to form and organise the army. In the view of Adam Smith the best way is to have a permanent standing army as the soldiers in an organised group where the soldiers are trained together they builds a team spirit and everyone is paid equally.

Need for Defence Budget in India

National Security is one of the paramount objectives of the Government and requires a comprehensive view of various political, social, economic, technological and strategic aspects. Defence policy making is one such part of overall National Security approach, but is more focused and concerned with the

---

7. L N Rangarajan,(1992), Kautilya: The Arthashastra, Penguin Books, p 117

protection of the state and its citizens from direct and indirect military threats and actions of other states.

But merely formulating policies and strategy is not enough. There should be proper economic resources to achieve aim of those policies. So, suppose the country has brought together the best defence strategists, who have come up with the best defence policy but unless the money is allocated against those policies, for its execution of those policies through capital acquisition or indigenous development or spending on R&D, there is no point of having strategies and policies. Hence it is important to allocate most favourable amount of resources in-order to strengthen our defence capabilities.

India is a federal country and Part XI- Article 245 to 255 of the Constitution of India provides for a division of legislative powers between the Centre and its states by dividing various matters of national interest into three Lists – Union, State and Concurrent. In this respect, Defence Services has been placed on the Union List (*Seventh Schedule – Article 246, Indian Constitution*) and thus comes under the legislative purview of the Central Government of India.[8]

It is the central government of India, which spends money on the defence services of India, thereby ensuring that we are safe. Expenditure of such a nature form part of the overall central government expenditure also known as public expenditure.

In today's time when the world is moving rapidly with technological advancement and economic rise, the need for more power and money is also increasing and with this is also advancing the need for physical expansion of nations to cater to the national interests. Hence, here comes the notion of expansion and capturing foreign land through use of defence forces. Apart from this in the 21st century the force is also used to project the power and might of a nation. Therefore, the defence forces are used not just for the protection but also for projection.

---

8. Basu D.D,(2005) "The Introduction to the Constitution of India", 19th Edition, New Delhi, Wadhwa and Company

India, which is a vast nation in terms of geography and demography, surrounded from all sides with nine neighbours. India has some difficult borders to manage and especially in the north with Siachen glacier being the most toughest and strategic post. The defence budget is required to resource and protract militaries and for financing these military activities both during war and peace time, with the training and upkeep of the equipments and other important tasks which we will discuss in later part. A separate proportion of finances in the name of defence budget are required.

Another prominent point is that role of defence forces are expanding everyday with large number of internal issues like environment protection, flood relief camps during natural calamities like typhoon, floods, earthquakes (Latur, Tsunami, Leh, Uttarakhand, Orissa etc),the blood donation camps. Now a day's defence is not restricted to fighting wars but it is also inter woven with social issues and also inter-organizational operations where the Army is together with local police in Jharkhand, Chhattisgarh and Northeast region fighting the Maoists and Naxals. The Air Force involved in providing food (air dropping) and airlifts of the casualties from the accident site to base. So it is observed that the role of defence forces has expanded over the years in all spheres both locally and globally by training the armies and navies of other countries and helping in establishing their organizations, also the United Nations Peace Keeping Force (UNPKF) where we are the largest contributors in terms of manpower. Hence, in order to produce so much of work and sustain itself the defence budget is undoubtedly required.

Analysis of the Defence Budget in India

Defence and defence expenditure is viewed as an uneconomical expenditure by some and as a zero profit organisation by others. The critics often argue that the expenditure on defence is incurred at the expenses of development. At some places the prominent economists have also quoted that the 'defence expenditure is very high and it affects the key areas like health care and education which requires massive investments'. The issues related to the defence sector in general and the defence budget in particular is not discussed adequately in our country. Due to this preposterous discussion there are innumerable misconceptions in the mind of common man and other economists regarding defence expenditure. This is due to the lack of awareness as far as the defence budgeting and process are concerned and also the too little information pertaining to the defence budget which is accessible to the public. It is true that unlike exhaustive data availability on union budgets and expenditure related to other ministries, restricted data (apart from annual reports and edited version) is made available in the public domain on the expenditure related to the defence sector. This kind of attitude many a times leads to the non admiration of the defence services in the society.

It is necessary to keep a watch and analyse the expenditure in order to review our own work and understand the shortfalls and more pressing needs for our organisation. In this way it can be tracked and make the organisation and its functioning more responsible due to which chances of malfunctioning becomes bleak.

This not only strengthens the organisation and its functioning but will also showcase the organisation as a responsible and duty abiding one.

However, the most important reason to analyse the defence budget is that it helps in assessing the military power. The trend in military expenditure indicates the strategic thrust and directions that the country seeks to pursue. It is vital to know the directions of not only of one's own country but also the one pursued by others, particularly the neighbouring countries in order to protect own national interests.[9]

9. Stockholm International Peace research Institute, "Monitoring Military Expenditures", http://www.sipri.org/research/armaments/milex/measuring-military-expenditures (Accessed in March 2013)

The quantum of defence budget also impacts the quality and morale of the military manpower in the form of personnel compensation packages, their living conditions and other welfare measures including welfare of their dependents in the family.

The method of formulation of the defence budget in India

The following chart explains the structure of Ministry of Defence and further explains how the budget is formulated.

Chart 1: Structure of Ministry of Defence

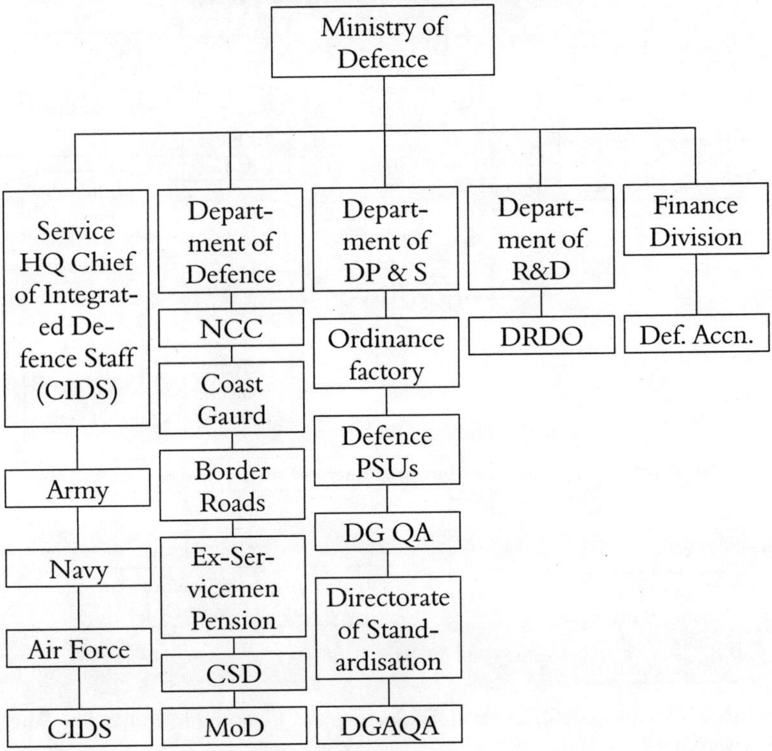

Source: (Ghosh, (2008), Defence Budgeting and Planning in India, p.47)

Role of Chief of Integrated Defence Staff

The Chief Integrated Defence Staff (CIDS) was created in the year 2001 for supervising and coordinating of plans for the key services and presenting a coordinated set of plans to the government. The Integrated Defence Staff is expected to function as a military filter to significant capital commitment being made in the plans and budgets. CIDS is therefore expected to give the inputs in the final stage of budget-making so as to act as a filter to the proposal regarding capital expenditure. On the basis of the role of CIDS as described in the budget documents, the flow chart below explains the budget formulation.

Chart 2: Budget Formulation Process

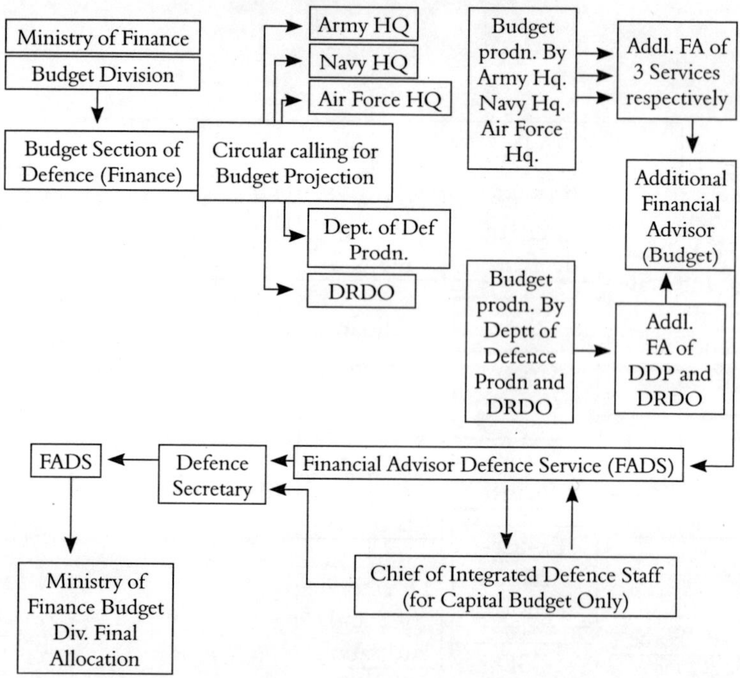

Source: Ghosh, (2006), Defence Budgeting and Planning in India: The Way Forward p. 83

As explained in the flow chart above, the formulation of the budget involves the down-up-down process involving projection of fund requirement by the lower formation to the higher formation for the forthcoming financial year (April 01 to March 31), in the mid way during the current financial year.

The Article 113 of the Indian Constitution requires that any expenses which are to be made on Consolidated Fund of India, needs to be voted in Parliament in the form of "Demands for Grants". It also draws distinction with the ones which are "charged" on the consolidated fund and need not be voted in parliament.[10]

Since, major part of the Defence Budget falls under the "voted" category; it needs to be voted in the Lok Sabah. Generally, one Demand for Grant is presented in respect of each ministry or department. However, in respect of large ministries like MoD, more than one Demand is presented.

The demands for grants of Ministry of Defence are of two types:

1. **Civil Estimates of Ministry of Defence –** This is for Ministry of Defence Secretariat
2. **Demand for Grants: Defence Services –** This is for the expenses of three services and includes both Revenue and Capital Expenses.

There are six Demands for Grants prepared for Defence Services. Five of them are for revenue expenses and one for capital outlay.[11]

In the case of the defence service the fund estimate is projected in the form of the Budget Estimate (BE) which is made by the units in the field which is then forwarded to the intermediary formation, who in turn consolidate the fund requirement for onward submission to the concerned Service Headquarters (SHQs) of the respective services (Army, Navy, Air Force).

Next the financial planning directorates of the SHQ merge the inputs from the lower formations and project the prerequisite to Ministry of Defence (MoD). The budgetary estimates put forward at the beginning of the financial year are subject to

10. Basu D.D,(2005) "The Introduction to the Constitution of India", 19th Edition, New Delhi, Wadhwa and Company
11. Defence Service Estimate Report, Ministry of Defence, Government of India

amendment during the course of the financial year to cater for shortfalls or excess requirements, if any. These are projected in the form of revised estimates (RE) by the SHQ to MoD.

On the receipt of the fund requirement under the revenue budget from the lower formation the specialist directorates of the three SHQs project the budgetary requirement to the MoD under the revenue and capital budget separately.[12]

The MoD and MoD (finance) authorities discuss the fund requirements projected by the SHQ and take up the estimate wished-for with the Ministry of Finance (MoF). If necessary the MoF which on the whole has the responsibility of government budgetary management may even prune such fund projection.

Finally the presentation of the union budget by the finance minister is made in the parliament and is approved afterwards. Post presentation the budgetary allocation to all the ministries is made by the MoF and then the allocation of the budget is made from top to bottom in a hierarchy by the MoF to MoD; further going down to SHQ initiates the process of sub allotment of the revenue budget to various lower formations, while retaining control over the capital budget.

Another important point to make note of is that the defence budget is divided into two major segments known as the "Revenue" budget and "Capital" budget. The division of the defence budget into revenue expenditure and capital expenditure is not only a constitutional requirement [Article 122(2)] but also an essential element for policy formulation and proficient resource allocation.

Revenue budget is undertaken by the graphically dispersed military units and other intermediate controlling formations. It is incurred for the purpose other than creation of assets for the central government. It denotes expenditure on upkeep and maintenance of physical assets and schemes. It also includes expenditure on

---

12. Srinivas V.N, (2008) "Budgeting for Indian Defence: Issues of Contemporary Relevance", New Delhi, K.W Publishers

pay and allowances, transportation, revenue stores (like ration, petroleum, oil lubricant (POL) and spares etc.) The financial power is delegated to the military commanders under the revenue budget.

The *Capital budget* is the one which leads to variations in physical assets of the government that is their acquisition, creation and disposal or additions, subtractions and alteration. It further includes expenditure on land, construction works, plants and machineries, naval fleet, aircraft and aero engines, heavy and medium vehicles and an omnibus classification called equipments. The capital budget takes place exclusively at the SHQ based on the requirements of the capital budget scheme that are likely to be taken up in the ensuing financial year. The reason for handling of the capital budget exclusively by SHQ has to do with delegation of financial powers. The financial power for approving schemes under the capital budget is vested only with the MoD.

It is necessary to understand the distinction between the revenue and capital categories of defence expenditure for two reasons.

Firstly, military modernisation is predominantly depends on procurement of technologically superior equipment for the armed forces. Military modernisation is a continuous process and the expenditure on account of all major new acquisitions is met from the capital budget. Therefore, the capital expenditure is significant and has a direct bearing on force modernisation. Similarly, Revenue expenditure is also important because a major portion of this category of expenditure goes towards meeting the pay and allowances of troops, which has direct impact on the morale of the military.

Secondly, understanding the attributes of these two categories would help in appreciating the government's budget management. To explain it further, the revenue deficit is the difference between revenue expenditure and revenue receipts. The revenue deficit indicates the excess of current expenditures over revenues or the no saving by the government, while the fiscal deficit captures the excess of overall expenditure over revenue. Revenue deficit implies increase in the liabilities of the central government without subsequent increase in the assets. So in this scenario when the aim is only to reduce the fiscal deficit, the brunt of fiscal alteration is often borne by reduction in capital expenditure. Therefore, by changing the ratio of the revenue and capital categories of the defence expenditure, the central government may at times, attempt to leverage the revenue and fiscal deficits to a certain extent, as required by the demands of overall government budgetary management.

Generally, higher the Capital-to-Revenue ratio is the more competitive and modern the armed forces are. Before 2004-05, India's armed forces had a C: R ratio of 27:73 but since then it has increased by about 12 percentage points to 39:61.[13]

The Capital-to-Revenue ratio is very different in the three armed forces. While the Indian Navy and the Air Force spend more than half their budgets on capital assets, the Indian Army spends less than 20% on average on capital. For example; in the financial year 2011-12, the Capital-to-Revenue ratio in army expenses reduced from a 17:83 in the budget estimate to 11:89 in the actual expenditure, implying that higher than expected revenue expenses were eating away at the already sparse capital funding.[14]

---

13. Srinath,(2013), The Transition State, "In Pragati: Understanding India's Defence Spending", http://catalyst.nationalinterest.in/2013/09/23/pragati-infographic-india-defence-spending/ (Accessed in November 2013)
14. Srinath, (2013) The Transition State, "In Pragati: Understanding India's Defence Spending", http://catalyst.nationalinterest.in/2013/09/23/pragati-infographic-india-defence-spending/ (Accessed in November 2013)

Chart: 3 Defence Planning to Formulation of Defence Budget by MoD

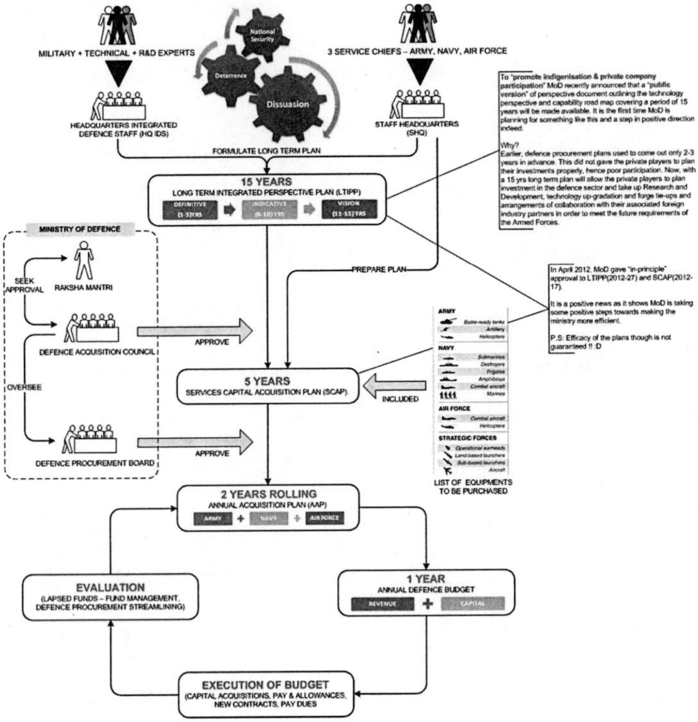

Source: Value of Dissent, (2012), "Public Expenditure and Defence Budget of India

Defence Services Estimates

One of the plausible features of the Indian defence budgeting system is that it is moderately transparent. The budgeted expenditure, revised estimates and the past actual expenditure figures are compiled in a document known as the volume of "Defence Services Estimates" (DSE) and is issued by the Ministry of Defence at the beginning of every financial year.

The entire defence budget of the central government is divided into major heads which is further sub divided into the minor heads, sub heads and code heads. Such a division facilitates accounting classification and identification. A detailed accounting classification is useful in projection of budgetary fund requirement, allotment of funds and monitoring of expenditure at all levels i.e. field units, intermediary controlling formations, SHQs, MoD and MoF.

As far as the Defence Services Estimates are concerned, currently there are six grants which are divided into six major heads, of which five major heads are for the revenue budget and one for the capital budget, as shown below.

Table 4: Outline of Defence Services Estimates

Serial No.	Demand No.	Major Head	Pertaining to
1	22	2076	Army
2	23	2077	Navy
3	24	2078	Air Force
4	25	2079	Defence Ordnance Factories
5	26	2080	Defence Research and Development Organisation (DRDO)
6	27	4076	Capital Outlay on Defence Services

Source: Defence Service Estimate Report, MoD, Government of India

The various minor heads and sub-heads contained in it do not indicate the details of procurement and resultant force capabilities. Nonetheless it is possible to ascertain the major items of expenditure such as manpower, stores, research and development (R&D), including unspent funds etc from this volume of DSE.

On the basis of the above structure, defence budgeting could be regarded as allocation of funds among the different functions, represented by six demands for grants, shown in the budget under six major heads of accounts.

Seen in this way, defence budgeting would appear as a major allocation exercise among the three Services and two departments of defence in the first tier of decision making relating to allocations of budgetary resources within the defence sector.

In the next tier of decision making within the funds allocated to a service, the budgetary exercise could be regarded as allotment of funds between revenue expenditure which basically caters for maintenance and operational preparedness and for capital outlay which caters for investment required for modernisation. Let us take the example of the budget for the year 2003-04 defence budgeting involved allocating Rs. 44,347.24 crore for revenue expenditure for the three services and two departments, which basically caters for maintenance of the defence force level and operational preparedness, and Rs. 20, 953.76 crore for capital expenditure which looks after the investment and modernisation expenditure.

From the budget allocated under capital outlay, one can find out how much is allocated for each service under this head. For example, out of total budget provision of Rs. 20,952 crore for capital outlay approximately Rs.6059.6 crore is for the Army, Rs.7413.6 crore for the Navy and Rs. 7478.6 crore for the Air Force. Thus one can understand and find out that how much is allocated for each service, under the revenue head and the under the capital head. The allocation can be graphically seen in the chart on the next page.

Chart 5: Function- wise Budget Allocation

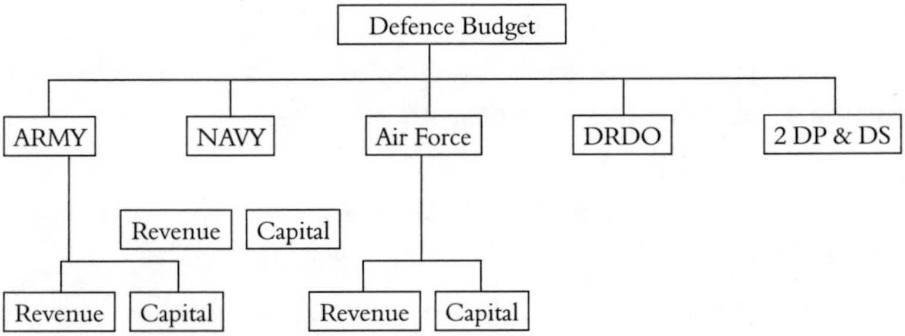

Source: Ghosh, (2006), Defence Budgeting and Planning in India: The Way Forward, p. 27

Allocation of Financial Powers and Utilisation of Funds

The important aspects that deserve examination are the authorities, be it in the armed forces or Ministry of Defence, who exercise financial powers in the utilisation of the defence budget, and the extent of such powers. The second important aspect that merits attention is the nature of expenditure itself.

These aspects are important as they help in understanding the system under which the defence budget is expanded and it also helps in getting to know the complexities and constraints surrounding the system, which otherwise is overlooked by our countrymen.

To begin with the defence expenditure of any country revolves around three major segments: personnel, maintenance and operations. The ministry of Finance and various authorities in the armed forces are delegated with financial powers. Until recently, the financial powers delegated to the armed forces were restricted to the revenue budget up to a limit. All financial approvals above the limit of Rs 10 crore under the capital budget will have to be accorded by the MoD up- to a certain laid down limit. Thus the financial powers are exercised by the authorities at various echelons in both the armed forces and MoD/MoF in respect of the capital and revenue budgets.

The armed forces are authorised to accord financial sanctions only in respect of cases falling under the revenue budget. Under this the major chunk goes into pay and allowances which is treated as an obligatory expenditure.

Here it is important to note that revenue cases beyond the delegated powers of the armed forces are referred to the MoD for sanctions.

The competent financial authorities (CFA) in the armed forces (authorities who are authorised to accord financial sanctions) are usually the commanding officers of self-accounting units and other staff officers of intermediate controlling formations such as brigade/division/corps/command headquarters and service headquarters.[15]

Linear Planning Process

The budget formulation and allocation is a multi layered/ tier process. Budgetary Allocation and Acquisition process is a part of the broad heading National and International Security Environment. There are various departments and sub departments that look into the threat scenarios and security strategy of our country and with the consultation and consensus formulate the National aim and Objectives. The defence Policies and Objectives are part of the larger category called the national aim which is formulated keeping in mind the protection of the territory from the adversaries. Once the defence policies and objectives to defend the borders and ensure the superiority in the technology is formulated the next step is to decide that what kind of military strategy should be adopted that can help us in achieving our objectives without making the cost of enforcement rise.

After the military strategy is formulated the next major step is to asses that what should be the force structure in terms of size, shape and composition. It also includes deliberation on the kind of weapons and equipment like guns, aircrafts, ships and their numbers.[16]

15. Srinivas V.N, (2008) "Budgeting for Indian Defence: Issues of Contemporary Relevance", New Delhi, K.W Publishers
16. Singh Jasjit, (2005) 'Aerospace Challenges for India' "Emerging India: Security and Foreign Policy Perspectives" ed., New Delhi, Institute for Defence Studies and Analysis and Promilla & Co., Publishers.

Chart 6: Linear Planning Procedure

National & International Security Environments

↓

Threat Scenario and Security Strategy

↓

National Aims and Objectives

↓

Defence Policies and Objectives

↓

Military Strategy

↓

Military Aims and Objectives

↓

Force Structure (Size, Shape and Composition of Force)

↓

Weapons & Equipment Assessment (types of weapon, Ships, aircrafts and their numbers)

↓

Strategic Military Plans (Employment/Position of Forces)

↓

Budgetary Allocation

↓

Acquisition Process (Buy, Buy with TOT, Build/Make)

Source: Ghosh, (2006), Defence Budgeting and Planning in India, p. 114

Once all this is deliberated and decided comes the most important aspect without which all the tires are ineffective is the budgetary allocation followed by the Acquisition Process (Buy, Buy with Transfer of Technology (TOT), Build/Make). This budgetary allocation and acquisition comes under a completely different organisation which is entitled to discharge its duties without any personal interests. This organisation will be discussed in our forthcoming chapters.

Chapter 3

Determinants of Defence Budget

Factors that determine the size of the defence budget primarily is (a) External and Internal security threat perceptions of the nation and (b) The resources available to meet these threats i.e. economic capability and hence it is an act of balancing in these two factors.

Defence budget determination is a complex process, this is because it involves the following aspects (i) analysis of geo-strategic environment, (ii) geopolitical compulsions (iii) geo-economic compulsions around the country, in the light of (iv) national values, (v) national objectives (vi) national interests. This kind of analysis gives a clear picture of the requirement of essential security of a nation. The national priority gives shape and size to defence budget.

The domestic environment of a nation has an important place in the security system of the nation state. For the holistic development of a nation in terms of economic, social, political and military capability is built from domestic security and resources. However there always exists the gap between the aspirations and satisfaction levels and this increasing gap is the threat to our security.

The security as a whole is derived from factors both at the internal and external levels. It also comprises of economic, diplomatic, political, social and cultural, technical and military attributes at national (internal) and international (external) levels. This means allotment of resources for defence/military is not merely economic process but it is also a part of the political bargaining process.

The size of defence budget in India is determined by economic capability, external security threat and internal or domestic security state of affairs. It is the duty of the institutions, actors, and process to assess the three perspectives and give shape and size of defence budget on the basis of available capital and aims.

Therefore, the resource allotment decisions for defence/ military/security are taken by evaluating the following three broad determinants-[1]

(a) *Internal Environment within the country* - political, social, technological and military factors and goals to be achieved.

(b) *External Environment around the country* - Foreign policy objectives of sub regional, regional and global levels.

(c) *Financial Capability* within the country.

In this way the levels of defence expenditure is determined at the focal point of influences from both international and domestic sources. The changes in national and international scenarios, threat perceptions, institutions (taking decisions) economic potential can bring about changes in defence expenditure levels.

The decision to allot the specific amount for each financial year on the security of the nation is based on the analysis of security environment fundamental national interests, evaluation of resources available and formulations of policy to deal with the threats.

Internal Environment

To begin with, in this chapter the internal security factor is discussed and how they drive the defence budget and hence are an important and crucial aspect in analysis of defence expenditure in our national context. It is vital for us to consider the matter of internal security in Indian context and analyse the problem

1. Athawale Sanhita,(2004), Defence Services, New Delhi, Anmol Publication Pvt Ltd

of internal security from the socio economic, political and other factors. We will also discuss and debate that how the internal matters have escalated over a period of time since independence.

There are numerable internal sources of threats that lead to tension within a nation and when any external support is received from the adversary country it adds to the problem of internal security. They are called as external factors of influences.

These sources which are internal and external in nature respectively are religious dissimilarities, ethnic dissimilarities, cultural dissimilarities, political inability, economic inabilities (high incidences of poverty and unemployment etc.) and political, industrial and criminal collusion.[2] The external factors of influence are different kinds of interventionist policies of super powers and their relations with the neighbouring countries, extra territorial loyalties of political and religious parties, aid to insurgencies by arms, money, organisation and instigation from others, and regional disputes, culture of terrorism at international level.

Although all the efforts are directed towards keeping a nation strong and successful but still it is difficult to achieve all round aspirations of a diversified society like India and this has led to the numerous internal security problems.

Some of the internal security issues that have been clinging to the Indian domestic history since its union till date are also some of the factors that suggest the importance of the strong defence system against the threats. As we probe into the internal situation we find that India is not being divided from within on various grounds. These internal security threats arise from terrorism, subversion, insurgency, secessionist movement in different parts of the country.

The ***Kashmir issue*** is one of the worlds known fact that is existing since 1947. The state of Jammu & Kashmir is facing 'Proxy War'

---

2. Lakshmi Y, (1988) Trends in India's Defence Expenditure, New Delhi ABC Publication House.

in some form or the other from the neighbouring adversary Pakistan. The state of Jammu & Kashmir is geo-strategically important from security point of view. It is continuing to face low intensity conflict in this region since 1948 with the infiltrators coming as local tribesmen, Pakistani nationals and foreign mercenaries in the valley for spreading militancy and terrorism.[3]

A study conducted by P. Stoban in 1996 states that, "out of total area of J&K 54.4% area is under control of China and Pak occupied Kashmir and 45.6% area is only under Indian control.[4]

Chart 7: J&K Area Inside and Outside Indian Territory

J&K Inside India	J&K Outside India
Jammu- 11.8% of total area.	8.9% of total area occupied by China.
Ladakh- 26.6% of total area.	15.3% of total area ceded to China by Pakistan for Karakoram Highway (KKH).
Kashmir- 7.2% of total area	30.2% of total area in Pakistan occupied Kashmir (PoK).

Source: Athawale Sanhita, (2004), 'Defence Services', p.204

As a result of such distribution various centrifugal stress and force operated in the state of J&K causing internal instability. To tackle these stress and conflicts the Indian Army has been conducting counter insurgency operations and is getting success since 1993. In this way the Kashmir issue has become a major internal security concern for India. But other than these external factors and active role of Pakistan in supporting terrorism deteriorates the internal security scenario.

One important thing to keep in mind is that these internal security threats revolves around its core values such as democracy, secularism, political instability, economic instability,

---

3. Athawale Sanhita, (2004), 'Defence Services', New Delhi, Anmol Publication Pvt Ltd
4. Ibid.

removal of poverty, and unemployment, equal rights, justice, self sufficiency in science and technology, religious and ideological freedom, protection of environment and security.

Another internal security matter that time and again has been on the priority list of the Indian government to make peace with is the ***North East Insurgency Movement.*** The insurgency movement in North Eastern Region (NER) i.e. Manipur, Tripura, Nagaland, Assam were initially treated as an extension of Chinese subversion but since 1970s the fight against insurgency is becoming more difficult in a democratic society and is creating unrest.[5]

Tripura: The Tribal National Volunteers (TNV) has stepped up the extremist activities and has intensified the violent activities. The TNV actions were supported by the Bangladesh and the Mizo National Front. The Tripura Government has used paramilitary forces and local police to control insurgency. Since 1998 the Central Government has stressed the need of central –State cooperation in dealing with insurgency. The new strategy now includes induction of more soldiers in Assam Rifles, redeployment of Army in trouble areas and parallel to this the government is trying to find out the political solutions.

Nagaland: The Naga Insurgency movement is based in the hill areas of Myanmar adjoining Nagaland and is functioning since 1956. They are fighting there war for the separate statehood for Nagaland through violent struggle. The problem of unemployment and poverty has helped the insurgents to strengthen their movement. The small group of politicians use these issues for extracting more funds in the name of development and misuse it, therefore, the political instability and underdevelopment is the main cause for this.

The Secessionist movement by the Gorkha National Liberation Front (GNLF) demanded the creation of autonomous

---

5. Athawale Sanhita,(2004), Defence Services, New Delhi, Anmol Publication Pvt Ltd.

Gorkhaland state in Darjeeling hills, which is a strategically important location from the security point of view on the Sino-Indian border and between Bhutan and Sikkim.

Similarly the Assam and Bodoland problem there has been an influx of foreigners from across the Bangladesh border continuously since independence. The issue started with the citizenship of these foreign nationals and their electoral rights. The root cause again for this is believed to be due to economic, social, cultural, and ethnic identity of Assamese people. Simultaneously the Bodo tribe dominated area in Assam started demanding for a separate state for Bodos. The United Liberation Front of Assam is demanding an autonomous Assam as a nation.

These insurgent groups from Nagaland, Manipur, and Mizoram, Assam get aid from across the border from China and Myanmar.

Another internal security threat that has off late gained large attention is the problem of ***terrorism***. India's internal security problems are aggravated by terrorism which has spread its web till the roots. Although these problems have domestic roots but the external factors gave impetus to these problems. Pakistan has been sponsoring and spreading armed violence through non-state actors and militants in the state of Punjab and Jammu and Kashmir, and slowly has also spread to the other parts of the country like the 26/11 Mumbai attack, Parliament Attack in New Delhi, Serial bomb blasts in Delhi, Bangalore, Varanasi so on and so forth. Although Pakistan denies its involvement in these accidents but the AL-Qaeda and other non state actor groups have always showcased there ideologies similar to Pakistani Aspirations and is funded by them. There are no two doubts about the Pakistani involvement and has been proved many a time in the international forums with dossiers and interrogation reports.

Therefore these are some of the threats to our internal security as a nation which are cause of socio economic failures as well as poor management by the Indian government.

Chart 8: Analysis of Internal Security Threats in India

Drivers	Basic Issues	Rising Demands	Major Threat to Security
POLITICAL	Political identity/sub-nationalism. Eg: Separate Jammu Movement since 1990. Demand of Buddhist Ladakhi for Ladakh Autonomous Council.	Separatist Movement and self Determination demand at Political level.	Militant/ Insurgency/ Sabotage terrorism.
SOCIAL/ CULTURL	Religion/Caste/ language And Other social problems. Eg: All North Eastern Region insurgencies since 1970-75. Bodoland, Gorkhaland, and Assam.	Religious identity formation. Integration on Social and religious basis, pressure group formation. North Eastern Region insurgencies in 1975-1985 and their talks and Assam accord.	Caste and Religious riots. Rise of fundamentalism and Communalism. Rising demand and continued activities of insurgent groups with external support since 1987.
ECONOMIC	Disparity in Development other economic problems. E.g. Jharkhand Movement in 1965 to 1975. Demands of all North eastern insurgencies since 1985 are focusing on economic disparities and economic backwardness.	Call for development Boards participation in economic process. Demands of Jharkhand co-ordination committee in 1988. Accepting economic bargains with government.	Militancy in economic demands strategies and external help. Continued demands of Jharkhand Mukti Movement. Militancy in economic demands since 1988.

Source: Athawale Sanhita S., (2004), 'Defence Services', New Delhi, Anmol Publication Pvt. Ltd, p.207

Role of Central and State Governments in Internal Security

In India the prime responsibility of the three Defence services is to uphold the sovereignty, territorial integrity and to undertake external security threats to the nation. This responsibility is equally shared by the police, the paramilitary forces and intelligence agencies of both the Central and State Government.[6] From the time of independence till date several paramilitary forces have been raised in India on an ad hoc basis to meet the requirements and immediate internal security challenges consequently the budget for paramilitary forces of the Union Government increasing from 1950-51 to till date.

The internal security in India is managed by the police, paramilitary and intelligence agencies of both Union and State governments. These agencies are charged with the responsibility of identifying, preventing, containing and eliminating threats to internal security. As stated earlier that these agencies are not cohesive and is not organised on any set pattern, therefore there exists a sort of mismanaged and under planned execution of decisions. Due to this the budget is not utilised in a well planned manner even when the amount is high.

At present there exists diversity in organisation in the agencies that are used to combat the threats to internal security of India and they also lack overall coordinating and controlling authority.

These paramilitary forces were raised in India in the 18thand 19thcentury essentially to extend the control of the British rule to the North Eastern part and North Western parts of the country at the minimum expenses. Some of the prominent paramilitary forces that are in existence till date and the role played by them is discussed in a tabular form below.

---

6. Ibid

Chart 9: List of Paramilitary Forces and the Area of Operation

Paramilitary Force	Area of Operation
Assam Rifles (AR)	Operates in North East region under operational control of Army. Works under Home Ministry.
Border Security Forces (BSF)	Patrols at the land borders of India in order to relive Army in peace time. It comes under Home Ministry in peace time and during war time it comes under the command of the Army.
Central Reserve Police Force (CRPF)	It enables the central government to intervene and police the trouble spots inside the country. It assists the State government, Army authority where they are operationally in charge of the internal security. This force also utilised in the relief operations in natural calamities.
Indo-Tibetan Border Police (ITBP)	It is for patrolling and policing the Indo-Tibetan borders in U.P, H.P, J&K sectors. Trained to carry out patrolling in high altitude.
National Security Guard (NSG)	This is a specialised force to combat terrorism in all forms and specialised in countering increasing terrorism in all forms.
Rashtriya Rifle (RR)	This force is used as an anti-terrorist force since 1991. It is a new para military force under the Ministry of Defence.
Coast Guard (CG)	It was formed within the Indian Navy for taking over peacetime duties in Indian Maritime Zone from Navy. It conducts general surveillance of Indian Coastline.
Police Force (PF)	Duty to maintain law and order in the nation.

Source: Athawale Sanhita, (2004), Defence Services, New Delhi, Anmol Publication Pvt P. 217

Internal Security Expenditure/Police Expenditure

For the understanding of the expenditure we undertake a trend analysis of the time period from 1973-74 to 1994-95 in four sections. We choose this period simply because we observe several internal security issues had come up.

(1) 1973-74 to 1979-80

In the first phase police/internal security expenditure grew at the exponential annual rate of 11.66 per cent. The North Eastern Region's insurgency movement was in a slow pace. The Assam problem was in the first level of the insurgency movement. The Punjab problem was posing an internal security threat, the evidence of Pakistan support was coming in forefront.

(2) 1979-80 to 1984-85

In this period the domestic security situation deteriorated and so expenditure on internal security was increased. In this phase the police expenditure had an exponential growth rate of 17.77 per cent per annum. The Punjab issue turned into a terrorist movement. The wide spread violence and terrorism prevailed in Punjab, Assam state. In 1984 Operation Blue Star was conducted when the army was sent inside the Golden Temple.

(3) 1984-85 to 1988-89

In this period the police expenditure was at 17.58 per cent per annum. The police expenditure continued to remain more or less the same as in the last phase which shows that domestic security threats remain dominant throughout the 1980s. Post Prime Minister Indira Gandhi assassination the internal security situation continued to put pressure on the expenditure on internal security during Prime Minister Rajiv Gandhi period.

In this period India was also involved directly involved in external problems like sending IPKF to Sri Lanka and that also cost India significantly.

The modernisation of police forces, acquisition of sophisticated equipments and creation of Rashtriya Rifle and National Security Guard was carried out during this period which further led to the build up of expenses on police.

(4) 1988-99 to 1994-95

The fourth phase witnessed slow down in the police expenditure as compared to the earlier phases as low as 16.00 per cent per annum. In 1990, the assassination of Prime Minister Rajiv Gandhi by LTTE human bomb created instability in political scene of India and the world witnessed international terrorism. India lacked major policy decision and during Narsimha Rao government in 1991 country went through economic crunch.

The economic crunch was the basic reason for the decreasing expenditure on internal and external security. The separatist movement of Jihad in J&K continued vigorously with the Pakistan support to jihadi movement. At the same time the dispute between the Cabinet Home Minister and State Home Minister on Kashmir issue took a toll and was highlighted. The Assam demand for Bodoland took a violent turn, the north eastern movement continued from insurgency to militancy.

Where as in Uttar Pradesh the demolition of Babri Masjid in 1992, created a rift between the two major religious fundamental groups; Hindu and Muslim of which the repercussion are still witnessed. The foreign exchange crisis continued but situation improvised under finance minister Manmohan Singh.

So in real terms India started facing problems of resources crunch and it has to slow down or overlook at certain internal threats which exists till date.

Conclusion

In India each state has its own peculiar law and order and internal security problems. Each state is authorised to have its own armed police forces. At the centre there are approximately fifteen to sixteen kinds of paramilitary forces which can be reinforced in any situation to assist and support the state government in handling the matters of internal security. However there is a managerial gap between central and state authorities, as well as the diversity in the agencies that are used to combat internal security challenges lack an overall control and coordination. Whereas the countries like China, Russia and Pakistan maintain paramilitary forces which are well integrated with their defence department. They are monitored and headed by the army or any other senior official from the defence department. This kind of inter services efforts help in creating a common understanding and also culture and values so that the amalgamation of military and paramilitary forces becomes automatic and helps in building cohesive team. India lacks this kind of coordination and successful execution of plans.

Instead of having so many paramilitary forces India should restrain from establishing various kinds of forces and should concentrate in training and establishing an inclusive force which can be utilised in some similar kind of challenges that India faces time and again. Also the paramilitary forces should be trained under the defence department in order to inculcate same values and culture for better understanding of each agency and smooth operation of tasks in hand.

External Environment

The external environment is the international environment in which a nation state pursue its national interests and national values, that presumably affects its military and other policies also. The external security environment is always analysed at three different levels: first; the global (Indian Ocean, Look West Policy and Look East Policy), second; the regional (ASEAN/SAARC) and third; the neighbours. The vastness of the country, its fluctuating economy, a 7600km long coastline, troubled neighbouring territories make India more vulnerable towards security and strategic threats.

In this section we discuss the external security environment that plays a role in determining the defence budget. We discuss the important factors in India's external security environment at the regional and global level.

India and the International Security Environment

Since the end of Cold War era there have been some fundamental changes in the global security scenario between the two super powers and bipolarity as it had been known since the end of Second World War. The new international world order that came in added another dimensions to India's security problems and has increased the sphere of potential conflict for the nation.

The disintegration of the erstwhile USSR has resulted in the loss of a friendly veto member of the United Nations Security Council for India. And the trade between the two nations started facing problems. The Gulf War 1991 (Iraq- Kuwait) demonstrated the technological supremacy of the West. As a result of the USA supremacy and presence in Gulf region will have its impact on the Indian security environment. The Islamic Fundamentals of Iran and internal problems of the neighbouring countries of India created threat for India.[7]

The process of economic globalisation was shrinking the world into one entity which has strangely enough broadened the parameters of security. Economic power and technological advancement became the prominent indicators of security along with military power. India adopted an economic restructuring programme in the 1990s in order to strengthen her economic position in world market before getting into the military build-up.

The rivalry between the two super powers continued to lay its impact on the international economic and political order. In this security environment the newly gained independence countries from Asia, Africa and Latin America were forced to join either of the two blocs. In the middle of all this the ideology and military power became important features and this led to increase in defence expenditure and defence acquisitions for security alliances for the developing country.

But few third world countries decided not to join any of the military blocs and retain their independence and chose the path of Non Alignment, India being one of the leaders of the Non Alignment Movement along with Yugoslavia, Egypt and

---

7. Ibid.

Indonesia. Therefore when the two super powers were busy in building the military blocs in the world India kept herself away from them.

India and Regional Security Environment

India being one of the major countries in Asia and specifically in South Asia has certain advantages but more of disadvantages in the region. Being geo strategically important nation it has been in the sour eyes of many neighbouring countries as well as it also posse's threat to some of the major powers as well.

The two most contentious nations that have influenced India's defence expenditure and foreign policy is Pakistan and China apart from some small level issues surrounding India. Since 1947 there is a permanent hostility between the two states stemming from territorial disputes, religious grounds, arms race, political aid, international alignments, regions role etc. In the initial years of independence India decided to concentrate more on the development than on defence and tried to assure its security through diplomacy.

India since beginning had issues with Pakistan and immediately entered into a conflict in 1948 on the Kashmir issue. Parallel to that India faced challenges from China and adopted the strategy of Panchsheel of peaceful coexistence. However the Panchsheel pact of 1954 proved a great failure as it ignored the geo-political compulsions and national interests of India. Later, in 1962 China attacked India over the border issues and in this 1962 debacle India got the reality check. It realised that non-alignment alone cannot help India in keeping its security issues under control. Along with well planned diplomacy India also required well thought-out defence plan and preparedness for the protection of the nation.[8]

Hence in the post 1962 period India tried to strengthen its defence capabilities and introduced many defence plans and re-

8. Lakshmi Y, (1988) Trends in India's Defence Expenditure, New Delhi ABC Publication House.

equipped military programmes. Therefore one observes rise in defence expenditure according to the then needs of security.

There were some other important developments in the global strategic horizons which affected Indian defence expenditure. With the growing ties between China and USA in 1971, it began to signal security threats for India due to nexus between Pakistan-China-USA against India. This strategic triangle between the three nations compelled India to turn towards USSR for support to its internal security aspirations. With the Indo-Soviet friendship treaty began a new era of economic and military cooperation along with weapon acquisition from Soviet Union to India.

In 1974 India tested its nuclear capability by carrying out its first underground nuclear explosion. This kind of nuclear status attained by India created serious concerns in the neighbouring countries and Western bloc. India's adversary Pakistan reacted to it with fast tracking its nuclear programme. The nuclear collaboration between Pakistan and China was brought to light soon after India rejected to sign the Non-Proliferation Treaty proposed by the Western Bloc.[9]

India and China both are the Asian super powers and are regarded as a competition amongst each other. China since beginning had global ambitions to be a world giant and due to that it always aimed at containment of India and having its influence in South Asia by establishing and maintaining closer ties with the neighbouring countries of India. This idea of China to have relations with nation which have bilateral problems with India brought Pakistan and China on the same platform. And this close relation between the two has always posed a grave security threat to India from a very long time.

Sino-India relations began to deteriorate since 1959 after Dalai Lama took political asylum in India; however Indian

9. Singh Jasjit, (2001), "India's Defence Spending: Assessing Future Needs", Institute for Defence Studies and Analysis and Knowledge World, New Delhi

leadership continued to ignore the alarming situations (when the Chinese army started patrolling on the McMahon Line in 1960. The year 1964 was landmark for the Chinese developed its nuclear capabilities and in 1980 China began its upgradation and modernisation plan of military power.[10] It has initiated a programme of reform in the military that would reduce its size but eventually increase its combat capabilities and led to qualitative improvement in standards. Simultaneously, understanding the international market China started strengthening its economic capability by promoting foreign investments in their country, liberalisation, international trade and expanding industrialisation.

Another major cause of concern for India from China and Pakistan is the issue of Siachen Glacier issue. The region has always been of strategic importance to the three countries. The Chinese interest in the region is that it provides a cushion to them and de facto occupation of Siachen by Pakistan would weaken any future Indian negotiations on border issues with China. And once the Indian position weakens the Pakistan occupation of Nubra Valley and Northern Ladakh and other routes going to Leh will be under threat. Therefore to avert any threat in the future it is imperative for Indian army to continue its commanding position and keep its military strength strong. Hence it requires huge expenditure on the defence of India in order to control the containment policy of China &Pakistan and not allows them to come further inside our country.

India and Other areas of Security Interest

Apart from China and Pakistan, India also has several other areas of concern in different parts. Some of the issues are discussed below.

"India will have to play a very great part in security problems of Asia and the Indian Ocean, more especially of the *Middle East* and *Southeast Asia,* as India is the pivot around which these

10. Kavic. Lorne (1967) "India's Quest for Security: Defence Policies, 1947-1965", Berkeley and Los Angeles, University of California Press.

problems will have to be considered." – Pt. Jawaharlal Nehru, The Discovery of India.

Indian Ocean

India is one of the important intertidal states in the Indian Ocean region. Almost the entire overseas trade of India is carried out through the Indian Ocean. It has always been a focus of the Indian diplomacy since Nehruvian era. Some of the reasons for the importance of Indian Ocean:-

1. Its value as a base from which forces located there could be suitably placed for deployment both within the Indian Ocean area and in the Middle East and the Far East.
2. A transit point for air and sea communications.
3. A large reserve of manpower of good fighting quality.
4. From the Northwest of which British air power could threaten Soviet military installations.

Therefore the Indian Ocean is considered at the conduit for Western military supplies. As a result the traditional maritime security concerns have become more important. Maritime security issues, including the protection of sea lines of communication.

With the coastline of 7000 km India occupies a dominating position in the Ocean. In the 1980 the USA has developed permanent presence of Rapid Deployment Force under its central command headquarters. The aim of the US base was to maintain nuclear deterrent against USSR. This automatically gave birth to Soviet interest in Indian Ocean in order to protect its national interests. And also to ensure its influence amongst the intertidal states it started exporting small arms to these countries.

In the 21st century the Indian Ocean has become a key strategic area. One of the reasons for this growth is increase in demand for raw material, including energy among the Asian economies for their growth. Also with the end of Cold War and the ongoing crises in Afghanistan and Iraq, the Indian Ocean is regarded as conduit for Western military supplies. As a result, traditional maritime security concerns have become more important. The security of chokepoints in the region the Straits of Hormuz, the Bab-el-Mandeb, and the Indonesian Straits has become a matter of great strategic importance for all the maritime powers.

Maritime security issues, including the protection of sea lines of communication (SLOCs), are paralleled by the increasing importance of the broadband communication connection between Asia, Europe and the United States that are linked with each other by the undersea cables traversing the Indian Ocean.[11]

New ports, roads, rail systems and pipelines now traverse Asia from West to the East and are making access between the landmass of Eurasia and the Indian Ocean intertidal much easier. This, in turn, will generate greater commercial traffic and the possibility for the greater strategic competition. The ongoing development by China of the Port of Gwadar in Pakistan is a matter of serious concern. Apart from strategic concerns the environmental crises in the Indian Ocean also needs due attention, with the forced migration and rising sea level and polluted sea water is a threat for all the surrounding countries specially India in the near future with the global warming at its peak. Along with this the over fishing in the Indian Ocean has caused depletion of marine life and it must be addressed soon.[12]

At present, about 25 percent of all oil used by the United States and 80 percent of crude oil imports used by China and Japan pass through the Indian Ocean. Consequently, the major powers now consider protection of this flow and sea-lanes of communication as a significant national priority.

---

11. Ajit Doval, (2012) "India's Internal and External Security: Areas that call for greater national attention", http://ajitdoval.blogspot.in/2012/09/indias-internal-and-external-security.html (Accessed in October 2012)
12. The Economist, "India as a great power Know your own strength" (March 2013) http://www.economist.com/news/briefing/21574458-india-poised-become-one-four-largest-military-powers-world-end. (Accessed in April 2013)

Hence for India to continue holding a strong position and also ensure regular peaceful trade through the Indian Ocean the government will have to certainly float in sufficient amount of funds to the defence and upgradation of maritime power for securing the national interests in the region.

Asian Neighbours: ASEAN, Look East Policy

India's Look East Policy was initiated in 1992 following the end of the Cold War and the start of the liberalization policy in which South East Asia and East Asia, especially the regional organisation, ASEAN, has been identified as central to India's policy in the Asia Pacific. According to Prime Minister Manmohan Singh "it was also a strategic shift in India's vision of the world and India's place in the evolving global economy." Consequently, increasing trade ties between India and SEA has contributed to the expansion of relations in the areas of defence and security. As a result, relations between India and the region have acquired strategic characteristics in recent years.[13]

India's increasing energy requirements and growing economic power have evinced New Delhi's augmented interest in the affairs of the Asia-Pacific Ocean.

With almost, 55 per cent of India's trade with the Asia Pacific transits through the SCS and India's maritime activities related to trade and exploration for hydro-carbons in the region and in particular in SCS in accordance with principles of international law have prompted India to look seaward—the Eastern Ocean—as part of its new version of LEP.

India being the largest power is likely to be a victim of the emerging power politics in the future, if not militarily equipped with the required strategic posture i.e. naval preparedness, technological self-sufficiency and readiness to accept a leadership role in providing the public good of maritime security.

13. Mayilvaganan, 'Examining India's Look East Policy 3.0', November,2013 http://www.internationalpolicydigest.org/2013/11/21/examining-indias-look-east-policy-3-0/ (Accessed on December 2013)

Also, Northeast can be used at the centre of country's Look East policy (LEP). India must start its development such as roads, telecommunication, and transit for facilitating trans-border trade having to pass through this region. Therefore, for the success of LEP, better cooperation and participation of North-East is needed.

India's Look West Policy

India has had its eye on Central Asia for a long time. Its primary interests there are in energy and establishing itself as a significant player in the interplay of outside powers that is taking shape.

Central Asia's rich energy resources and India's persistent energy needs, combined with India's aspiration to be a major regional and global player, have been the key driving forces behind India's growing presence in the region. India's involvement in Central Asia includes energy ties, trade and investment, and the beginnings of a military relationship. Diversifying and expanding its international sources of energy has been a major Indian policy thrust for the past decade, so it is no surprise that energy co-operation is at the heart of India's engagement of Central Asia.[14]

Outside the energy area, transportation infrastructure is a major focus, since poor transport links are a major obstruction in order to expand economic ties. India has made significant contributions to the trans-Afghan roadway and railroad. India is also interested in the future North-South trade corridor, which if it is completed would make road linkages from the Iranian port of Chabahar through Afghanistan into Tajikistan.[15] It has also signed a deal to fund an Iran-Turkmenistan-India roadway. This infrastructure development will not only serve the economic demands of India but will also give impetus to its strategic policies in this region.

14. Pradhan K Prashant, (2011), 'Accelerating India's Look West Policy in the Gulf', , (Accessed on December 2013)
15. Singh Roy, Meena and Lele, Ajay (2011) 'Engaging Iran in the New Strategic Environment Opportunities and Challenges for India', Strategic Analysis, 35, New Delhi , IDSA

Even the Prime Minister of India has launched a "look west" policy to improve its ties with the Gulf countries.[16] Many of the Gulf Countries senior officials interact with the Indian Defence organisation and are being trained in the various military academies at different levels. They agree on having high level high military exchanges, joint training of the troops and joint naval exercises by the navies in the Red Sea and in the Persian Gulf.

In December 2006 India signed a strategic Memorandum of Understanding on Defence Cooperation with Oman that included exchange of expertise in military training and information technology, utilization of military and educational courses and programs, exchange of observers attending military exercises and exchange of formal visits.[17]

Apart from the aforesaid areas India cannot and must not ignore its immediate neighbours in the sub continent. Its relation with Nepal, Bhutan, Bangladesh, Sri Lanka and Myanmar will always be the key to its aspiration of the world leader and also torch bearer of peace and tranquillity. And in this region India also faces challenges from China who are executing fast and also well planned policies for their future goals. Especially Nepal and Bhutan is the epicentre of the conflict at the moment as China is signalling its interest in Arunachal Pradesh.

Therefore India should increase its military level interactions with these countries in some form or the other with the aim to win their heart and mind.

Financial Capability

The financial landscape in India continues to go through rapid changes both in terms of the greater responsibility towards the country and to manage financial well-being of the consumers/

---

16. Pradhan K Prashant, 'Accelerating India's Look West Policy in the Gulf', February 2011, (Accessed on December 2013)
17. Ibid.

citizens and the greater complexity and variety of tools and financial products available in this effort.

Managing finances is a complex set of challenges in the best of the times, requiring a combination of skills, judgment and resources. In today's volatile economic environment, the challenges are especially acute and the downside risks are great. The country must fight with incomprehensible variety of financial decisions, ranging in vast area. Even the simplest of these decisions requires at least some basic financial knowledge and competency, while the more complicated decisions are challenging even for experts.

Financial capability cannot be measured simply by looking at one indicator, such as demonstrated knowledge of specific terms or concepts. Instead, financial capability encompasses multiple aspects of behaviour relating to how a country manages their resources and how they make financial decisions. It is a multi-dimensional concept that requires looking at vast set ups from various angles.

Conclusion

Allocation problems arising in the defence sector concern the division of inputs between immediate production of military goods and long term investment, the choice between better quality and larger quantity of military goods, choice of different types of weapon models, inter-service allocations of military goods etc. The allocated resources for defence can be misused due to lack of co-ordination, misdirection or misinformation and may lead to wastage of productive resources.

Also it must be remembered that decisions necessarily do not always flow from national values downwards, but rather resource constraints affect policy objectives and even in some cases national values. This is based on the requirement approach where certain issues emerge with sudden change in the security environment and these situations cannot be assessed or funds can not determined in advance for such changes. Since the change in domestic or international security scenario can have its impact on the defence spending.

Jasjit Singh points out that "There also appears to be a time gap between the formulation of the national plans and corresponding defence plans. This disjunction needs to be made efficient and relevant."[18]

18. Singh Jasjit, (1996), 'Defending India in the 21st Century: issues of affordability and credibility', Strategic Analysis, Vol. XIX No. 7, New Delhi

Chapter 4

Trend Analysis of Defence Budget Since 1950

This section will focus on the trend of India's defence budget in four phases from 1950 -1970 and 1971 – 1990, followed by another two phases in next section.

It is a universal truth that the economic capability is an important factor and this capability in the real sense provides resources for the defence sector. There are some important elements of the national security like the military security, political security, cyber security, protection of natural resources and energy environmental security, and to ensure all this security the most important element is the economic capability.

In today's complex system of international trade, characterised by multi-national agreements, mutual inter-dependence and availability of natural resources etc., the freedom to exercise choice of policies to develop a nation's economy in the manner desired, invites economic capability. Economic capability today forms, perhaps, as important a part of national security as military security. Therefore in order to ensure that all the elements of national security are fulfilled we need finances to achieve our targets and hence defence is broadly based on the economics of a country.

Before analysing the defence expenditure it is imperative to understand the background of the country during period of independence. India awoke to its "tryst with destiny" with a chronic deficiency in its ability to feed itself. The Great Bengal

Famine had occurred mere four years before independence. India would continue to import food grain for its people for two decades after British left. The Green Revolution was still two decades away. In fact, this gave rise to the term living a "ship to mouth" existence because if a ship-load of wheat from United States did not dock in our ports, tens of thousands of people could have died. [1]

With this brief background, it was inevitable for the country to not look into the issues toward socio- economic development even if it were to be at the cost of defence. But, as it is a well known truth that defence was not seen as a major challenge in the early years. This was a prevalent thought during the first 15 years; however this perspective still dominates thinking in important decision making circles. During that time it was felt that the requirements of development were paramount and there was no alternative to adjusting defence policy to this priority.[2]

Now going to the trend of the defence expenditure of India we observe that by 1950, the country had formally initiated efforts at planning for accelerated growth consistent with the objective of social justice. In India's first Five Year plan (1951-56) the focus was laid on agriculture, price stability, power and transport. Therefore during the first five year plan the defence expenditure was held somewhere between 1.62 to 1.52 percent of Gross Domestic Expenditure (GDP) and around 31.90 to 18.20 of the Central Government Expenditure (CGE).[3]

In his book Lorne J. Kavic "India's Quest for Security: Defence Policies, 1947-1965" has mentioned that before 1962 war with China Pdt. Jawaharlal Nehru in his speech mentioned that how development of defence is not the primary goal for India in the wake of independence. In the aftermath of China's occupation

1. Singh Jasjit, (2001), Defence in the Past, India's Defence Spending, New Delhi, Knowledge World international.
2. Ibid.
3. UPSC Guide.com, Summary: Five Years Plan in India, http://www.upscguide.com/content/summary-five-year-plans-india (Accessed in January 2014)

of Tibet in 1950-51, at least a section of the Army leadership was convinced that it would be sensible to form a small specialized force to maintain a constant surveillance of the Himalayan frontier. Political disinterest and Nehru's order to drop any such proposal, was with this belief that the Chinese military threat to India's Himalayan frontiers and the interests in the hill states was distant and should not be stimulated by any Indian actions or attitude that might be regarded by them as provocating.[4]

In 1954 the Himalayan situation began to deteriorate and there was an increasing concern in the military circle and refusal by the political authorities to appreciate the need for the phased adjustment. Later in 1960 Chief of Army Staff visited Italy to make a study on the Alpine troops of Italy and on his return he made certain recommendations to the Indian government through Defence Ministry. The proposal was however rejected by the government. Both the Defence Minister Menon and Prime Minister Pdt. Nehru seems to have felt that the formation of such a divisions would constitute a shift in the strategy with far reaching and unwelcome repercussions on foreign policy. The cost of such measures according to them would increase the country's already heavy defence burden. Instead the government of India in their second five year plan (1956-61) focussed on the rapid industrialization and shifted emphasis from agriculture to industry and advocated huge imports through foreign loans.[5]

The country's GDP at in 1956-61was 3.36 percent and the share of defence expenditure was 1.03 percent of the GDP and 21.5 percent of the CGE. In this period not much was done in terms of build up the potency of the defence forces both in terms of the manpower and weapon modernisation.

Even after 15 years of independence till 1962, the Indian Defence organisation continued to be based on the imperial British military system the weapons and ancillary equipment of the Army dated from World War II and, in some cases ,before.

4. Kavic, Lorne (1967) "India's Quest for Security: Defence Policies, 1947-1965", Berkeley and Los Angeles, University of California Press.
5. Ibid.

Communication system was old and suited for static condition. The vehicles were generally old and well-worn and 15 percent of jeeps, 38 percent of three ton general service trucks and 68 percent of the one ton general service type were acquired before 1948. Hence, for the contingency of the Himalayan operations against China the services were ill-prepared.

As a result post 1962 war till 1970-71, the defence budget had accelerated and the defence budget was average between 2.56 to 3.84 percent of the Gross Domestic Product (GDP) and 20.14 to 25.63 percent of the Central Government Expenditure (CGE). In the year 1963-64 the CGE rose to 25.45 percent and 3.84 percent of the GDP which is increase of 63.98 percent from the previous year which is also said to be the step taken after the Sino-India war of 1962.[6]

On the other hand, after appearance of a recognizable Chinese threat to India's security and also deteriorating relation between India and Pakistan. Neither country made serious efforts to improve its relations in the aftermath of the Sino-Indian border conflict, and tension was heightened by an increasing number of violations of the ceasefire line in Kashmir, by clashes between Indian and Pakistani troops in the disputed Rann of Kutch and in Kargil area and within 22 days an undeclared war between the two countries in 1965.[7]

In the year 1965 when India witnessed a war with Pakistan the defence expenditure for the fiscal year 1965-66 was 3.38 percent of GDP and 22.45 of CGE. The budget was only 8.98 percent more from the fiscal year 1964-65 when it was 3.25 percent of GDP and 23.1 percent of CGE. However in the financial year there was a further dip in the budget from maximum 3.38 percent of GDP to 2.73 percent in the year 1969-70 and 25.63 percent of the Central Government Expenditure.[8]

6. Mathews Ron, (1989) Defence Production in India, New Delhi, ABC Publication House
7. Lakshmi Y, (1988), Trends in India's Defence Expenditure, New Delhi ABC Publication House.
8. Singh Jasjit,(2001), 'Defence Expenditure Trends', India's Defence

India was mostly importing its defence equipments from there only friend in the Cold War era the USSR. Soviet Union offered its assistance to India during several issues like the Liberation of Goa in 1961 and also extended its support by vetoing a resolution on the issue of Kashmir.

In 1962 during the Sino Indian conflict Soviet Union extended support to India and even offered to cooperate with India in the manufacture of MIG Fighter planes in India. Soviet Union also signed an agreement for the supply of arms and military hardware to India. It continued to be the biggest supplier of tanks, bombers, aircrafts, and artillery and radar equipments to India.[9]

The defence budget for the nation during 1965-71 was maximum 3.38 percent and minimum 2.80 percent of the GDP. In this period the five year plan of central government focused on agriculture, self reliant and self generating economy. The GDP of the nation during this period was around 2. 93 per cent.

It is important to note that apart from our defence and security several other issues which were of equal importance and similar urgency. However, due to lack in decision taking capability of our leadership ended in a continued slow progress till date. And it poorly affected our defence modernisation plan, even after consistent persuasion by the military chiefs.

By the year 1970 two pay commissions had came in implementation the first pay commission was constituted in May 1946 and was based upon the idea of "living wages" to the employees. Whereas, the second pay commission was set up in August 1957, it had the financial impact of 396 million rupees.

It may be recalled that the period 1962-1970 was marked by two major wars (1962 and 1965) and two major arms clashes after China acquired nuclear weapons (Rann of Kutch in 1965, and Nathu La in 1967). Besides many other factors, the wars and

---

Spending, New Delhi, Knowledge World International

9. Lakshmi Y, (1988), Trends in India's Defence Expenditure, New Delhi ABC Publication House.

corresponding sense of insecurity, especially after the traumatic defeat of 1962, no doubt had an effect in the negative figures in the wake of two wars, while the growth rate in 1962-63, the year of Sino Indian war, was down to 2.12 percent as compared to the average of 4.99 percent for the five years period spanning.[10]

Historically, the defence expenditure has been substantially low to 1.62 percent of the GDP for the first 12 years following India's independence, which has often been cited as one of the reason for the loss in the 1962 war with China. As a result, money for the defence had been forthcoming at an average annual rate of 3.05 percent of the GDP for last 25 years. And economic growth appears to have accelerated since then. Access to Soviet sources of defence equipment since early 1960s for bulk force needs was another major factor in providing a fairly high degree of military capability at low costs.[11]

The correlation of the GDP growth rates and defence spending indicates that increase in defence spending seems to have coincided with the higher GDP growth rates. At the same time, it is worth noting that the defence expenditure as a proportion of the CGE has been coming down in successive years.

Based on this correlation of GDP of India and defence expenditure, it could possibly be said that defence spending in India has an overall positive impact on economic growth, as reflected in the GDP growth rates.

Table 10: Defence Budget Share of the GDP and CGE 1950-70

Year	Defence Budget of GDP (%)	Defence Budget of CGE (%)
1950-51	1.62	31.90
1956-57	1.52	18.20
1960-61	1.52	14.50
1961-62	1.83	21.33
1962-63	2.56	20.14

10. Ibid.
11. Ibid.

Year	Defence Budget of GDP (%)	Defence Budget of CGE (%)
1963-64	3.84	25.45
1964-65	3.25	23.1
1965-66	3.38	22.45
1966-67	3.07	20.38
1967-68	2.8	21.53
1968-69	2.82	22.83
1969-70	2.73	25.63

Source: Awasthi, (2014), 'Trend in India's defence Budget 1950 – till Date', India's National Security in the 21st Century, 2014, p. 507

Phase II

In the second phase of this chapter, the defence expenditure trend from 1971 – 1990 will be elaborated. This phase was marked by a moderate flow of the defence expenditure. Although in the year 1971, India faced challenge of a war with Pakistan on the issue of East Pakistan. There was a steady decline in India's defence budget falling back to 2.48 percent of the GDP in 1966-70. It again rose to 3.02 percent of the GDP of the 1970-71 the year of war with Bangladesh and remained at 2.96 percent in 1972-73. In this period the Indian economy was recovering from 1971 Bangladesh war effects. From 1973 to 1986, the defence expenditure was within the range of 2.46 and 2.87 percent of the GDP. The declaration of Emergency in 1975, the defeat of Congress party and prime minister Indira Gandhi in 1977. General election also contributed to the moderate defence expenditure. Some changes were expected in defence policy, planning, international relations with other countries, economic policies, and nuclear policy etc. during this period.[12]

In 1980 Indira Gandhi came back to power. India was stabilised

12. Joshi Praveen (2005) 'India's Defence Expenditure: Historical Perspective', Emerging India: Security and Foreign Policy Perspectives, Ed. New Delhi, Institute for Defence Studies and Analysis and Promilla & Co. Publishers

as regional power in South Asia since the 1971 war and has created adequate defence and dual purpose infrastructure in the decade after the war. Indian economy also recovered. But the security environment continued to deteriorate further both at international and domestic level.

Although the defence establishment had been growing during the first 15 years of the period after 1963, subsequent mechanisation and modernisation of the early mid 1980s which caught up with the neglect of 1970s may explain the increase in the defence expenditure. Moreover this also happened during the period when the value of the rupee dropped by over 70 percent as compared to the US dollar. Thus, what we were facing is prolonged erosion of defence expenditure since the mid-1980s which was basically due to increase in the manpower cost and the force level had not altered. Its spill over effects was on the capital expenditure, equipment and non-manpower stores being neglected.[13]

A closer examination of the defence expenditure reveals that, contrary to conventional wisdom, manpower costs had started to rise by the early 1970s.[14] The rate of growth of manpower costs (excluding pension) had started to increase at an average annual figure of around 14.85 per cent by the late 1980s.

By 1986-87, the expenditure had moved up to 3.6 percent of the GDP, primarily because of relatively higher costs of weapons and manpower.[15]

Another main factor for this apparently sharp growth were the higher costs of force modernisation, as also the recommendation of fourth and fifth pay commission in the year 1973 and 1983 respectively. As noted earlier, the cumulative effect of the implementation of the fourth pay commission was an increase

---

13. Singh Jasjit, (2001), 'Defence Expenditure Trends', India's Defence Spending, New Delhi, Knowledge World International.
14. Singh Jasjit, (2001), 'Manpower Optimisation', India's Defence Spending, New Delhi Knowledge World International.
15. Singh Jasjit,(2001), 'Defence Expenditure Trends', 'India's Defence Spending, New Delhi, Knowledge World International

of 10.74 percent in pay and allowances and similarly was the case during fifth pay commission. This also implies that unless defence spending increase at a higher rate of interest, available allocation of reequipment, training and maintenance will continue to be inadequate. On the other hand India's defence debt, especially from Russia, should be reducing in the coming years unless additional debt is added on through purchase of equipments and weapons.

The implementation of the recommendations of the fourth Central Pay Commission had resulted in 107.48 percent increase (since January 1996) in the direct cost of manpower in the defence services due to the increase in pay and allowances. It may be recalled that the recommendation of the Third Central Pay Commission had also resulted in increase of defence spending in 1974-76.[16]

The GDP growth rate seems to have been significantly higher in the 1980's when defence expenditure was also rising continuously. The year 1986-87, 87-88 marks the highest ratio of defence expenditure as percentage of GDP in the whole period.

The increase was due to various reasons. A few of them can be summarised as- "in 1984 the operation 'Blue Star' was conducted with the help of military to control the terrorist activities from the Golden Temple in Amritsar, Punjab. The internal security problems in this period took serious turns all over the country. This was followed by the assassination of Prime Minister Indira Gandhi in 1984. Internal disturbances grew and threatened to tear apart the fabric of Indian system. The political instability was revived by giving the leadership to Rajiv Gandhi. He vigorously continued the modernisation programme of defence sector and started adding sophisticated weaponry to Indian arsenal. More expenditure was diverted towards technology upgradation, research and development. [17]

16. Ibid.
17. Lakshmi Y, (1988), 'Trends in India's Defence Expenditure', New Delhi, ABC Publication House.

At the international level external threats from Pakistan, China, and Indian Ocean region continued. India sent Indian Peace Keeping Forces (IPKF) in 1987 to Sri Lanka to resolve ethnic issues which had its repercussions into the Indian Territory.

This period witnessed four major war-like situations. They included the localised war in Siachen, Jammu and Kashmir with Pakistan and the border skirmishes in Arunachal Pradesh. Along with this the external support from Pakistan, China, Bangladesh, Nepal continued for internal separatist movement which caused increase in internal security expenditure.

The defence expenditure on revenue account increased during the year 1987 due to implementation of the fourth Pay Commission's recommendations and subsequent revision of pay and allowances of the armed forces. Therefore the defence expenditure for the year 1987-88 under revenue head and capital head was 8891.61 cr and 3099.21 cr respectively which is 31.17 percent increase from the previous financial year. Whereas, the defence expenditure in terms of GDP was 3.34 percent and CGE was 17.53 percent.[18]

In the post fourth pay commission period from 1987-88 to 1994-95 witnesses a sharp decline in the growth rate of defence expenditure. This decline had various reasons, the most important being that Indian economy started facing grave problems. The resource crunch led to these defence expenditure cuts.[19]

Table 11: Defence Budget Share of the GDP and CGE 1971-90

Year	Defence Budget of GDP (%)	Defence Budget of CGE (%)
1970-71	2.78	21.51
1971-72	3.3	22.73

18. Singh Jasjit,(2001), 'Defence Expenditure Trends', 'India's Defence Spending, New Delhi, Knowledge World International
19. Athawale Sanhita, (2004), 'Defence Services', New Delhi, Anmol Publications Pvt. Ltd

Year	Defence Budget of GDP (%)	Defence Budget of CGE (%)
1972-73	3	21
1973-74	2.53	20.4
1974-75	2.69	21.25
1975-76	2.93	19.96
1976-77	2.82	18.75
1977-78	2.56	16.98
1978-79	2.57	15.28
1979-80	2.74	17.69
1980-81	2.47	15.82
1981-82	2.53	17.13
1982-83	2.62	16.4
1983-84	2.62	16.4
1984-85	2.83	16.18
1985-86	2.83	15.16
1986-87	3.32	16.64
1987-88	3.34	17.53
1988-89	3.14	16.86
1989-90	2.95	15.51

Source: Awasthi Soumya, (2014),' Trend in India's Defence Budget 1950- Till date', India's National Security in the 21st Century, 2014, p. 510

Trend Analysis of Defence Budget: Part III

In continuation to the above discussion, here the defence budget for the next two phases from 1990- 2010 and 2011- 2014 will be discussed.

The average annual growth for the following decade in the 1990s declined to 11.96 percent as compared to 20.92 percent for the decade 1988-1997. It should have been increased due to the inevitable increase in the cost of replacement of weapon systems. For example the MiG-21 combat aircraft at US$ 1 million cost Rs. 1.1 crore in the mid 1970s. A new combat aircraft replacing the MiG-29 acquired in 1990s was for around US$ 18 million apiece.[20]

The inflation level in the country continuously remained in double digit in this period from 10.3 to 13.7 and it affected real term expenditures. Also the devaluation of money in the year 1991 which meant 24.58 rupees against 1 USD, added to the inflation.

India faced critical situation on the economic front. Liberalisation, privatisation, globalisation measures were taken for restructuring the Indian economy. The foreign exchange reserves condition was the worst in the Indian history since independence during 1990.

In the political area instability continued after the assassination of Prime Minister Rajiv Gandhi in 1990. The internal security threats continue to be dominant. Jammu and Kashmir experienced low intensity warfare supported by Pakistani aid. At the international level sea changes occurred which have long term effects on the Indian security. The end of cold war brought the issue of ideology to the end and the economic issue has acquired primacy over all other issues. The international economic conditions led to the shrinking of the word resources and debt trap continued to pose great threat to international security.[21]

The process of Soviet disintegration lost an important friendly ally to India. India lost its easy access to military technology and weapon systems. Rouble-Rupee trade was also affected badly. Indian armed forces started facing problems of spare parts for its weapon system.

India tried to develop its relations with the United States and collaborate in areas of defence and economy. However, India did

20. Singh Jasjit,(2001), 'Defence Expenditure Trends', 'India's Defence Spending, New Delhi, Knowledge World International
21. Athawale Sanhita, (2004), 'Defence Services', New Delhi, Anmol Publications Pvt. Ltd

not get similar helps as it expected and was going through some serious economic crisis and so it could not allocate adequate resources for defence.

The capital expenditure has been the main subject of fluctuations in defence spending over the years due to change in currency exchange ratios and further by inflation. In other words, it is the modernisation, re-equipment and replacement of obsolete weapons and equipment that is affected most by major fluctuations/cutbacks in defence budget. Average annual growth rate of capital expenditure during the quarter century after 1962 was 16.17 percent.

The defence expenditure as a proportion of the GDP declined markedly from 3.50 percent in 1987-88 to 2.09 percent for the financial year 1996-97.

Table 12: Defence Budget Share of the GDP and CGE 1990-91 to 1996-97

Year	Defence Budget of GDP (%)	Defence Budget of CGE (%)
1990-91	2.86	14.64
1991-92	2.49	15.52
1992-93	2.83	14.33
1993-94	2.53	14.33
1994-95	2.28	14.65
1995-96	2.25	15.06
1996-97	2.14	14.67

Source: Awasthi Soumya, (2014),' Trend in India's Defence Budget 1950- Till date', India's National Security in the 21st Century, 2014, p. 515

Unfortunately the low rate of growth of capital expenditure during the 1990s has had a serious negative impact on the defence modernisation and preparedness. To some extent, this could be explained by the fact that new acquisitions did not require this period. The 'Bofors syndrome' appears to have played a strong restraining role. Above all the absence of war and preoccupation with internal security possibly affected thinking at all levels. The cumulative effect of not sustaining re-equipment on a steady basis has resulted in virtually no modernisation during the 1990s and somewhere in the early years from the year 2000 onwards.[22]

Table 13: Defence Budget Share of the GDP and CGE 1997-98 to 2000-01

Year	Defence Budget in GDP (%)	Defence Budget in CGE (%)
1997-98	2.26	15.2
1998-99	2.27	14.28
1999-00	2.36	15.24
2000-01	2.38	14.79

Source: Behera Laxman, (2000), 'India's Defence Budget', IDSA p.2

The average defence expenditure was pegged at 16.48 per cent of Central Government expenditure during the decade of the 1980s. This share came down to 14.63 per cent in the next decade up to the turn of the century. Similarly, defence expenditure as a ratio of total (Central plus state) government expenditure came down from 10.5 per cent during the 1980s to 7.75 per cent during the 1990s, a period during which the rupee depreciated against the dollar from about Rs 16 to a dollar to Rs 46 to a dollar. Taking inflation of seven to eight per cent also into account, the defence budget declined in terms of constant rupees by over 10 per cent per annum.

It was pretty clear in 1964 that India's security was affected by the nuclearisation of its environment when China acquired nuclear weapon and similarly in the year 1987 when Pakistan acquired a nuclear weapon as well. However in 1998 India following China and Pakistan declared its nuclear status. During 1998-99 the

22. Athawale Sanhita, (2004), 'Defence Services', New Delhi, Anmol Publications Pvt. Ltd

defence expenditure of India was 2.27 percent of the GDP and 14.28 percent of the CGE Consequently; this led to a decline in India's conventional defence capability and preparedness for war and emboldened Pakistan to launch its ill-fated intrusions into the Kargil sector of Jammu and Kashmir in May 1999.

The year 1999 holds lot of significance in the history of Indian military. In this year the country went through tough time with the war between India and Pakistan famously known as the Kargil War. A year before the Kargil War the country's defence budget was 2.27 percent of the GDP and 14.28 percent of the CGE. The Service wise budget allocation was around 68.51, 9.06 and 19.34 percent for the Army, Navy and Air Force respectively. [23]

A historical analysis of allocations since independence reveals that except for the three years each in 1960s and late 1980s and two years in early 1970s, the defence expenditure has remained below 3 percent of GDP. Moreover, the defence allocations have even gonebelow two percent of GDP as recently as in 2007-08 (see table below). This has evoked concerns among many, including the Parliamentary Committee, which recommended to the government to provide "a minimum 3 percent of GDP" to fulfil, among others, "the need based requirements of the Defence Forces".[24]

Table 14: Defence Budget share of the GDP and CGE 1989-90 to 2008-09

Year	Defence Expenditure as % of GDP	Defence Expenditure as % of CGE
1989-90	2.97	15.52
1990-91	2.27	14.65
1995-96	2.25	15.06
2000-01	2.36	15.24
2005-06	2.32	15.91

23. Ibid.
24. Behera Laxman, 2000, 'India's Defence Budget', New Delhi, IDSA

Year	Defence Expenditure as % of GDP	Defence Expenditure as % of CGE
2006-07	2.16	14.64
2007-08	2.03	14.11
2008-09	1.95	14.06

Source: Awasthi, India's National Security in 21st Century, 2014, p. 511

While it is indisputable that Defence Services need to be adequately funded and higher percentage of GDP would lead to that, the question is whether defence's declining share in national output implies the governments shifting priority of resource allocation. Considering that, the defence budget is completely funded by the Union Government, the former share in total CGE shows governments intentions as far as resource allocation is concerned. As above table shows the share of defence in CGE in last 20 years does not reveal a clear declining trend, rather some fluctuations, with the share of defence accounting for about one seventh of GE for most of the years.

Indian defence spending in last 20 years between 1989-2008-09 has increased substantially, from Rs.14, 416.17 to Rs. 1, 05,600 crores. This represents average annual growth of 11.5 percent. The growth of India's defence expenditure is however not so even. The highest annual growth was recorded in 2004-05 when the expenditure was increased by Rs. 15,790.12 crores, representing a growth of over 25 percent. The lowest growth in absolute term was in 1991-92 with an annual increment of Rs 920.56 crores. In percentage terms the lowest growth was in 2002-03 when spending was increased by merely 2.57 percent.

The defence budget for the year 2007-08 was 96,000 crore which is merely 2.03 percent of the GDP and 14.11 percent of the CGE as compared to the budget for the year 2006-07 of Rs. 86,000 crore. In the new budget, Revenue expenditure accounts for 56.3 percent and Capital expenditure for 43.7 percent of the total budget. Compared to the revised estimates for 2006-07, in the latest allocations, the share of revenue expenditure has decreased by 3.6 percent while that for a capital expenditure has gone up by the same percentage points.[25]

The recent trend of declining revenue allocations and rising capital allocations can be traced back to 2004-05, when the capital budget was suddenly increased by nearly one and a half times, while the revenue budget was cut by nearly 14 percent. When the recommendations of the 6th pay commission got implemented, the revenue budget will inflate significantly. The 5th pay commission inflated the revenue budget by nearly 16 percent. A similar situation this time will raise the revenue budget by at least eight to nine thousand crore, because of increase in just Pay and Allowances.[26]

The defence budget for 2007-08 is only 2.10 percent of the expected GDP for the coming fiscal year, as against 2.17 percent in the previous year. In the last four fiscal years since 2004-05, Defence expenditure as a percentage of GDP has been continuously declining. Similarly, Defence expenditure as a percentage of total Central government expenditure has this time around come down to 14.11 percent from 14.79 percent in the previous year. in nominal term though the economy is all set to grow by more than 45 percent between 2004-05 and2007-08, the defence budget has actually gone up only 26 percent in the same period.

A perusal of the Defence Service Estimate (DSE) reveals that the Armed Forces surrendered nearly Rs. 40,000 crore in the past decade, forgetting the consequences of two important underlying principles of the Fiscal Responsibility and Budget Management Act (FRBM Act) each rupee surrendered from the present budget is one rupee lost in the next budget.

For the year 2008-09 the government of India allocated 105,600 crores for India's Defence. For the first time, it crossed the one

25. Behera Kumar, Laxman (2012), ' India's Defence Budget 2012-13 'http://www.defencereviewasia.com/articles/169/India-s-Defence-Budget-2012-13 (Accessed in August 2012)
26. Ibid.

lakh barrier and accounted for nearly 14.1 percent of total Central Government Expenditure (CGE) and 1.99 percent of the Gross Domestic Product (GDP). It was increased by 10 percent over the previous year's allocation of Rs. 96,000 crore. In the last five years, the defence budget has increased by nearly 37 percent in 2004-05, which represents over 8 percent growth per annum. The economy registered an average growth of nearly 8 percent a year during 10th plan, and continued the growth momentum in the 11th plan period. This testifies to the fact that the economy is much more globalised that, say, 10 years ago when trade accounted for less than 20 percent of GDP.[27]

A survey of the regional military balance shows India's unfavourable position vis-a-vis its neighbours. China's relentless military modernisation, backed by double-digit growth in military expenditure for more than a decade, is a case in point. Given the above imperative and the moderate nature of India's defence spending, the question arises as to how much India should spend on defence.[28]

In terms of proportion of economic resources devoted to defence, India's latest defence budget, which accounts for 1.99 percent of expected GDP in the coming Fiscal Year is less than the global average of around 2.5 percent, and lags behind America's 4.1 percent and Pakistan's 3.5 percent. In absolute terms, India's defence spending ranked 10th in the list of major spenders in the world constitutes a fraction of the American military budget and less than half of China's budget for 2008.[29]

---

27. Awasthi Soumya, (2014) 'Trends In India's Defence Budget 1950-Till date', India's National Security in the 21st Century, ed., New Delhi, Pentagon Press
28. Masters, Jonathan,(Nov 2011), 'Defence Spending and Deficit Debate', Council on Foreign Relations, http://www.cfr.org/defense-budget/defense-spending-deficit-debate/p26442 (Accessed in January 2013)
29. The Economist,(March 2013), "India as a great power Know your own strength" http://www.economist.com/news/briefing/21574458-india-poised-become-one-four-largest-military-powers-world-end. (Accessed in April 2013)

The defence budget for the financial year 2009-10 has increased by 3.19 percent over the previous year's budget estimate (E) of Rs. 1,05,600 crore. In this year the budget was 2.3 percent of the GDP and 13.88 percent of the CGE.

The revenue expenditure has been increased to more than 61 percent in comparison to its last year's share of less than 55 percent. The growth if capital expenditure had declined, over the previous year's growth to 14.20 percent. The faster growth of revenue expenditure is primarily due to the hefty increase in pay and allowances flowing from the implementation of Sixth Pay Commission (CPC). To put the figure in perspective, total budgeted pay and allowances debited from the services budgets has more than doubled from 21,891.67 crores in 2008-09 to 44,500.69 crore in 2009-10.[30]

The Fiscal Year of 2010-11 witnessed a modest growth of 3.98 percent in the latest defence budget, in comparison to 34.19 percent in 2009-10. The relatively smaller growth in the defence budget is reflected in its declining shares in the gross domestic product and the total central government expenditure. Among the services, the Army, the biggest consumer of the defence budget, has witnessed a noticeable decline, in terms of its percentage share in defence budget, whereas the Air Force has been the major beneficiary in the budget 2010-11.

The Navy has almost held on its last years share. The Air Forces increased share has largely been due to enhanced budgetary provision under the head of capital expenditure. The over and above last year's allocation can be seen in the context of its planned induction of medium multi-role combat aircraft (MMRCA). One noticeable change in the latest budget pertains to the ratio between revenue and capital expenditures. In comparison to previous year, the share of capital expenditure in the overall budget had increased to nearly 41 percent.

30. Singh Jasjit, (2001), "India's Defence Spending: Assessing Future Needs", Institute for Defence Studies and Analysis and Knowledge World, New Delhi

As the defence budget 2010-11 reveals, the Ministry of Defence surrendered Rs. 5,439 crore from its budget of 2009-10. It is noteworthy that in last five years, the defence ministry has surrendered over Rs. 24,218 crore from its total budgeted capital outlays, with annual unspent amount varying between Rs. 2,037 crore around 6 percent and Rs. 7,089 crore approximately 15 percent.[31]

For the financial year 2011-12 the union budget allocated 1.83 percent of the GDP and 13.07 percent of the CGE. It was an 11.59 per cent growth over the previous year's budget, which was remarkable for two reasons. Firstly, the defence budget has not been unduly impacted by the government's fiscal consolidation process. Secondly, the defence budget shows, at least on the face of it, the MoD ability to spend the resources, particularly the capital portion, within the stipulated time.

On the revenue side, although the growth has been necessitated by the increase in the pay and allowances, there has also been an increase in the budgetary provision for other revenue its such as stores, transportation, etc.

The adequate increase in the defence budget has had a favourable impact on key statistics, except in terms of its share in total central government expenditure and GDP. The declining share of defence in these key parameters can be ascribed to the relatively faster growth of the Indian economy and the resultant increase in total central government expenditure. On the positive side, the ratio between revenue expenditure and capital expenditure has improved in favour of the latter, showing greater focus on the modernisation plans for the Army, navy and Air Force. However among the three services the Air Force received largest share for the acquisition followed by Army and Navy.

It is noteworthy that the large provision under the capital acquisition budget is for some major items like the C-17

31. Behera Kumar, Laxman, (June, 2012) ' India's Defence Budget 2012-13, 'http://www.defencereviewasia.com/articles/169/India-s-Defence-Budget-2012-13 (Accessed in August 2012)

Globalmaster, Advanced Helicopters for army and air force, patrol vessels and for the previous year plan for Medium Multi-Role Combat Aircraft (MMRCA).

In the year 2011-12, total pay and allowance of the three services and the DRDO estimated to grow by 10.3 per cent. This represented 54.2 percent of the total revenue expenditure and 31.4 percent of the total defence budget; it is also responsible for 28 percent of the increase in the total defence budget.

It is to be noted that pay and allowances are obligatory in nature and the government has no control over their growth, given the mandatory increase in annual pay and allowances. Moreover, most of today's pay and allowances constitutes tomorrow's defence pensions. The growth in these two sections always had great impact on the other spheres of the defence budget.

The union budget2012-13 hiked the defence outlays to Rs.1, 93,407.29 crore. This represented a growth of 17.63 percent over the previous year's outlay. It was one of the highest increases excluding the 2009-10 when the budget increased to 34 percent, mostly to accommodate the implementation and recommendations of the 6th Central Pay Commission.

This budget came at the time when the Indian economy was going at all-time low and the scope of recovery seemed to be flimsy. As the Economic survey 2011-12 mentioned GDP growth rate of the nation is projected at 6.9 percent and at 7.6 per cent in 2012-13 respectively. Unlike the revised estimate for 2010-11, in which both the Revenue Expenditure and Capital Expenditure were higher than their respective budget estimates, the revised estimate for 2011-12 showed an increase in Revenue Expenditure and decline in Capital Expenditure. From the perspective of resource allocation, while the share of the defence budget in the GDP had marginally increased to 1.90 percent as compared to 1.83 of 2011-12, its share in Central government expenditure had fallen to 12.97 from 13.07 percent of 2011-12.[32]

32. Awasthi Soumya, (2014) 'Trends In India's Defence Budget 1950-Till date', India's National Security in the 21st Century, ed., New Delhi, Pentagon Press

It is worth mentioning that compared to the budget for the year 2011-12, Navy was the only service which has increased its share in total defence allocation from 15 to 19 percent. The Air Force's share had decreased by 4 percent whereas the Army's share had declined by 1 percent. A closer look at the budget of 2012-13 will reveal that the entire focus of modernisation was on the Navy followed by marginal increase in modernisation budget for Air Force and lastly Army which witnessed decline by 3 percent.[33]

For the year 2013-14 the Ministry of Finance allocated the defence budget as 1.79 percent of the GDP and 12.23 percent of the CGE which was 5.3 percent increase from the previous year. It was considered as a nominal increase in the budget allocation compared to growth rate of 17.6 percent and 11.6 percent in the last two years budget of 2011-12 and 2012-13 respectively.

However the reason for such a budget was the economic slowdown, high inflation and an adverse rupee-dollar exchange rate. Due to this government was forced to tighten its purse. This step taken by government was evident from the growth rate of both the union budget and the defence budget while the former has increased by 11.7 percent; the increase in the latter is less than a half of that. In other words the budget was callously controlled not only in the interest of the larger fiscal deficit, but also to accommodate the relatively larger shares of other expenditures of the government.

Of the total cut in the capital expenditure, around 87 percent is due to what generally is known as under spending of the modernisation budget, which has been reduced by 13 percent. Therefore around 75 percent of this is accounted for by the Navy whose modernisation budget has been reduced by 26.9 percent due to slippage of delivery of the Air Craft carrier INS Vikramaditya by almost a year to late 2013 (November). This decline in the defence budget as a part of GDP due to economic

33. Ibid.

slowdown was considered to be lowest over the past five decade since 1961-62 when it was only 1.66 percent.[34]

In this fiscal year 2012-14 the Indian armed forces were on a grand modernisation process with Air Force having contract for 126 French Rafale fighter jets to be delivered in the 2014-15 financial year, 22 Boeing AH- 64D Apache Longbow attack helicopters, 15 Boeing CH-47 F Chinkoo heavy lift helicopters and 6 Airbus A 330 Multi Role Tanker Transport. The Navy was also expected to sign contract for 16 multi role helicopters and the Army on its part is hoping that its much delayed artillery programmed finally gets going in 2013, with the procurement of 145 ultra light howitzers.[35] However, due to economic growth there are hiccups in modernisation plan, with little room for new schemes.

Finally, coming on to the trend analysis of the India's Defence Budget we will discuss the interim budget that was presented in the Parliament by the Finance Minister on 23rd February 2012. The Interim Union Budget 2014-15 allocated Rs. 2,24,000 crore, it represents a 9.98 percent increase over the 2013-14 defence budget is exclusive of Rs. 53,582.15 crore for defence pension that includes 500 crore on account of the governments acceptance of the armed forces long standing demand for One Rank One Pension (OROP) principle. Although the interim budget is relevant only till the new government is not formed in the centre and a regular budget is not presented post general elections this year.

The increase in the pay and allowances is also the main reason for bulk of the hike in the interim defence allocations. Suffice to

---

34. Ajit Doval,(Feb2012), 'India's Defence Production and Research – Need for Transformational up-gradation', http://www.vifindia.org/article/2012/february/06/India-s-Defence-Production-and-Research-Need-for-Transformational-up-gradation. (Accessed in Feb2012)
35. The Economic Times, (November 2008) 'India's Ten Latest Defence Procurement Programmes', http://economictimes.indiatimes.com/indias-10-latest-defence-procurement-programmes/slideshow/3694983.cms (Accessed in August 2012)

mention that in the new budget, 48 percent of the total increase is accounted for by the hike in armed forces salary component. Compared to this, the Capital expenditure, which mainly caters to the modernisation requirement of the armed forces, has contributed to only 14 percent of the total hike.

Among others, it brings out clearly that although the growth of the interim budget is higher than that of the previous year's budget, the growth as mentioned earlier is consumed by swelling revenue expenditure. Consequently, the capital expenditure, its growth and its share in total defence budget cut an unimpressive outlook. This year's interim budget shows share of defence budget in GDP is 1.74 percent as compared to 1.80 percent and the share of defence budget in CGE is 12.70 percent in contrast to 12.23 percent of 2013-14.

In spite of the 10 percent increase in the overall defence expenditure, there has been a marginal increase in the capital acquisition budget of the armed forces. Of the three services Army is only wing to get the hike in its modernisation budget much of its growth is however concentrated on 'Other Equipment' which caters to missiles and artillery gums. This may give an opportunity to Army to sign its long delayed procurement deals of ultra-light howitzer, Javelin anti-tank guided missile and night vision equipment.

In comparison to Army, both the Navy and the Air Force have witnessed a decline in the capital acquisition budget, with latter bearing a heavy brunt. Given that its budget has been reduced drastically, it is now very unlikely that the Air Force could sign this much talked about fighter deal in 2014-15, which is awaited since January 2012.[36]

Hence, leaving very little to meet the modernisation requirements, particularly of the Indian Air Force, which has numerous

---

36. Behera Kumar, Laxman, (June, 2012), ' India's Defence Budget 2012-13, 'http://www.defencereviewasia.com/articles/169/India-s-Defence-Budget-2012-13 (Accessed in August 2012)

pending deals for signing. From a long term perspective what is of more relevance is that given the continuous steep rise in the pay and allowances of the 1.4 million strong Indian armed forces, the pressure on the modernisation would be felt more acutely in the coming years. This is more so, given the prevailing poor economic outlook, increasing subsidy bill, growing demand from social sector on Union Budget, and limited fiscal space available with the government.[37]

Expenditure of Defence Budget

Table 15: Defence Expenditure in Gross Domestic Product (GDP) and Central Government Expenditure (CGE) (1950- Present)

Year	Defence Expenditure in GDP%	Defence Expenditure in CGE %
1950-51		
1951-52		
1952-53		
1953-54		
1954-55		
1955-56		
1956-57		
1957-58		
1958-59	1.83	21.33
1959-60	2.56	20.14
1960-61	3.84	25.45
1961-62	3.25	23.1
1962-63	3.38	22.45
1963-64	3.07	20.38
1964-65	2.8	21.53
1965-66	2.82	22.83

37. Ajit Doval, (Feb2012),"India's Defence Production and Research – Need for Transformational up-gradation", http://www.vifindia.org/article/2012/february/06/India-s-Defence-Production-and-Research-Need-for-Transformational-up-gradation. (Accessed in Feb2012)

Year	Defence Expenditure in GDP%	Defence Expenditure in CGE %
1966-67	2.73	25.63
1967-68	2.78	21.51
1968-69	3.3	22.73
1969-70	3	21
1970-71	2.53	20.4
1971-72	2.69	21.25
1972-73	2.93	19.96
1973-74	2.82	18.75
1974-75	2.56	16.98
1975-76	2.57	15.28
1976-77	2.74	17.69
1977-78	2.47	15.82
1978-79	2.53	17.13
1979-80	2.62	16.4
1980-81	2.62	16.4
1981-82	2.83	16.18
1982-83	2.83	15.16
1983-84	3.32	16.64
1984-85	3.34	17.53
1985-86	3.14	16.86
1986-87	2.95	15.51
1987-88	2.86	14.64
1988-89	2.49	15.52
1989-90	2.83	14.33
1990-91	2.53	14.33
1991-92	2.28	14.65
1992-93	2.25	15.06
1993-94	2.14	14.67
1994-95	2.26	15.2
1995-96	2.27	14.28

Year	Defence Expenditure in GDP%	Defence Expenditure in CGE %
1996-97	2.41	15.79
1997-98	2.36	15.24
1998-99	2.38	14.79
1999-00	2.26	13.46
2000-01	2.18	12.74
2001-02	2.4	15.22
2002-03	2.32	15.91
2003-04	2.16	14.64
2004-05	2.03	14.11
2005-06	1.95	14.06
2006-07	2.3	13.88
2007-08	2.12	13.29
2008-09	1.83	13.07
2009-10	1.9	12.97
2010-11		
2011-12		
2012-13		

Source: Reserve Bank of India, Annual Reports

Table 16: Budget Abstract of Army (1950-Present)

Year	Share of Army (Cr)	Army Budget (%)
1950-51	143.57	80
1951-52	139.75	77.1
1952-53	148.1361	76.86
1953-54	145.8632	73.04
1954-55	140.65	71.02
1955-56	125.68	67.91
1956-57	134.55	66.61
1957-58	161.79	61.02
1958-59	154.64	58.15

Year	Share of Army (Cr)	Army Budget (%)
1959-60	147.36	60.7
1960-61	174.83	65.77
1961-62	204.24	67.66
1962-63		76
1963-64	550.77	77.73
1964-65	548.59	76.54
1965-66	569.79	74.1
1966-67	618.05	74.71
1967-68	638.08	74.48
1968-69	699.39	74.12
1969-70	709.93	72.49
1970-71	725.12	69.73
1971-72	875.03	70.09
1972-73	986.46	70.25
1973-74	1,063.31	68.55
1974-75	1,349.00	69.11
1975-76	1,486.67	67.83
1976-77	1,593.43	67.11
1977-78	1,642.20	66.03
1978-79	1,638.75	63.28
1979-80	1,802.92	59.89
1980-81	2,094.04	59.83
1981-82	2,465.95	59.63
1982-83	2,821.86	58.72
1983-84	3,441.36	60.34
1984-85	3,997.70	62.74
1985-86	4,627.88	66.92
1986-87	6,069.60	67.7
1987-88	6,865.60	77.21
1988-89	6,846.42	72.28
1989-90	7,446.64	72.51

Year	Share of Army (Cr)	Army Budget (%)
1990-91	7,962.73	72.33
1991-92	8,131.42	70.93
1992-93	8.769.42	70.97
1993-94	10,231.96	68.52
1994-95	11,335.87	68.28
1995-96	12,927.38	68.66
1996-97	14,145.40	67.47
1997-98	18,349.78	68.51
1998-99	22,067.77	71.18
1999-00	26,645.07	74.3
2000-01	28,614.63	72.13
2001-02	29,602.89	73.95
2002-03	29,608.88	72.08
2003-04	28,264.70	65.16
2004-05	28,914.83	63.04
2005-06	30491.64	
2006-07	32,169.57	62.44
2007-08	34,202.60	62.44
2008-09	48,178.21	65.47
2009-10	76,679.70	88.26
2010-11	74,589.79	85.36
2011-12	83,415	87.6
2012-13	97,302.54	85.48

Source: Defence Service Estimate, Annual Reports

Table 17: Budget Abstract of Navy (1950-Present)

Year	Share of Navy (Cr)	Navy Share (%)
1950-51	8.21	4.75
1951-52	8.27	4.56
1952-53	10.19	5.28
1953-54	10.975	5.49

Year	Share of Navy (Cr)	Navy Share (%)
1954-55	11.23	5.67
1955-56	11.09	5.99
1956-57	12.69	6.28
1957-58	14.76	5.56
1958-59	16.06	6.03
1959-60	15.38	6.33
1960-61	18.26	6.86
1961-62	19.4	6.42
1962-63		
1963-64	22.67	3.19
1964-65	22.35	3.11
1965-66	28.14	3.65
1966-67	34.69	4.19
1967-68	37.97	4.43
1968-69	39.81	4.21
1969-70	45.21	4.61
1970-71	56.23	5.4
1971-72	65.54	5.25
1972-73	69.85	4.97
1973-74	96.08	6.19
1974-75	97.8	5.01
1975-76	128.62	5.86
1976-77	150.66	6.34
1977-78	170.19	6.84
1978-79	168.48	6.5
1979-80	203.59	6.76
1980-81	225.49	6.44
1981-82	302.37	7.31
1982-83	375.38	7.81
1983-84	484.87	8.5
1984-85	492.69	7.73

Year	Share of Navy (Cr)	Navy Share (%)
1985-86	569.07	8.22
1986-87	668.28	7.45
1987-88	683.7	7.68
1988-89	773.9	8.17
1989-90	829.85	8.08
1990-91	825.8	7.5
1991-92	941.84	8.21
1992-93	993.83	8.04
1993-94	1,278.15	8.56
1994-95	1,436.89	8.65
1995-96	1,831.56	9.72
1996-97	2,048	9.76
1997-98	2,429.01	9.06
1998-99	3,136.69	10.11
1999-00	3,593.81	10.02
2000-01	4,024.61	10.14
2001-02	3,862.03	9.64
2002-03	4,357.77	10.61
2003-04	4,908.21	11.31
2004-05	5,296.99	11.81
2005-06	18.08	
2006-07	6,810.67	13.22
2007-08	7,090.82	12.94
2008-09	8,032.56	10.91
2009-10	20,604.00	23.71
2010-11	21,467.50	24.5
2011-12	25,246.89	26.51
2012-13	37,314.44	32.78

Source: Defence Service Estimate, Annual Reports

Table 18: Budget Abstract of Air Force (1950-Present)

Year	Share of Air Force Rs. In Crore	Air Force Budget (%)
1950-51	12.72	7.08
1951-52	18.77	10.36
1952-53	19.2	9.96
1953-54	27.65	13.84
1954-55	30.86	15.58
1955-56	34.03	18.38
1956-57	41.93	20.75
1957-58	75.29	28.39
1958-59	82.07	30.86
1959-60	64.07	26.39
1960-61	58.58	22.03
1961-62	59.49	19.71
1962-63		
1963-64	135.06	19.06
1964-65	125.48	17.49
1965-66	148.67	19.33
1966-67	151.06	18.26
1967-68	155.58	18.16
1968-69	175.72	18.62
1969-70	191.37	19.54
1970-71	214.45	20.62
1971-72	259.08	20.75
1972-73	292.88	20.85
1973-74	333.29	21.48
1974-75	397.58	20.37
1975-76	466.31	20.28
1976-77	515.8	21.72
1977-78	540.81	21.75
1978-79	626.8	24.2

Year	Share of Air Force Rs. In Crore	Air Force Budget (%)
1979-80	814.44	27.05
1980-81	919.96	26.29
1981-82	1,047.65	25.34
1982-83	1,226.11	25.51
1983-84	1,325.93	23.25
1984-85	1,445.55	22.69
1985-86	1,718.27	24.85
1986-87	2,093.42	23.35
1987-88	1,655.55	18.62
1988-89	1,780.20	18.8
1989-90	1,855.34	18.06
1990-91	2,072.61	18.83
1991-92	2,333.96	20.36
1992-93	2,532.70	20.5
1993-94	3,367.51	22.55
1994-95	3,771.14	22.72
1995-96	3,911.20	20.78
1996-97	4,375.43	20.87
1997-98	5,180.33	19.34
1998-99	5,512.20	17.78
1999-00	6,518.32	18.18
2000-01	7,293.33	18.25
2001-02	7,014.70	17.52
2002-03	7,417.40	18.05
2003-04	7,845.59	18.08
2004-05	8,506.32	18.97
2005-06		
2006-07	9,865.59	19.15
2007-08	10,352.32	18.9
2008-09	12,198.91	16.58

Year	Share of Air Force Rs. In Crore	Air Force Budget (%)
2009-10	34,432.26	39.63
2010-11	40,462.45	46.3
2011-12	46,151.78	48.47
2012-13	48,191.16	42.34

Source: Defence Service Estimate, Annual Reports

Table 19: Defence Budget Revenue Expenditure and Capital Expenditure (1950-Present)

Year	Revenue Expenditure (Cr)	Capital Expenditure (Cr)	Inc. Over Last Year
1950-51	179.46	5.75	5.97
1951-52	181.24	16.15	13.42
1952-53	192.72	8.71	11.38
1953-54	199.68	10.36	0
1954-55	198.02	13.08	3.97
1955-56	185.06	20.4	0.76
1956-57	201.98	21.23	2.31
1957-58	265.13	24.88	19.97
1958-59	265.93	27.83	10.46
1959-60	242.74	36.44	-9.74
1960-61	265.8	36.2	12.56
1961-62	301.82	25.5	1.59
1962-63			50.49
1963-64	708.51	115.63	72.21
1964-65	716.69	117.85	-1.26
1965-66	768.94	119.23	9.8
1966-67	827.17	114.86	2.69
1967-68	856.7	112.86	6.59
1968-69	943.53	107.3	6.69
1969-70	979.22	125.32	6.55

Year	Revenue Expenditure (Cr)	Capital Expenditure (Cr)	Inc. Over Last Year
1970-71	1039.79	142.74	8.94
1971-72	1248.28	162.36	27.19
1972-73	1404.03	195.42	8.32
1973-74	1550.96	201.69	1.73
1974-75	1951.79	204.72	25.67
1975-76	2191.46	218.08	17.04
1976-77	2374.3	240.23	3.65
1977-78	2486.68	264.31	2.77
1978-79	2589.57	254.69	8.88
1979-80	3010.11	261.56	17.02
1980-81	3499.48	296.87	15.23
1981-82	4134.95	460.32	20.3
1982-83	4805.35	540.47	16.26
1983-84	5703.14	582.75	16.66
1984-85	6371.44	758.95	13.11
1985-86	6915.23	939.44	11.93
1986-87	8964.62	1203.44	31.17
1987-88	8891.61	3099.21	14.22
1988-89	9471.17	3714.25	11.48
1989-90	10268.7	4223.33	8.06
1990-91	11008.54	4731.21	7.01
1991-92	11463.05	4877.4	5.97
1992-93	12356.11	5132.54	7.55
1993-94	14931.56	6548.08	24.25
1994-95	16601.93	6926.21	6.41
1995-96	18826.01	8033.59	15.53
1996-97	20964.52	8506.85	9.86
1997-98	26782.98	9281.64	19.57
1998-99	30998.86	10171.42	16.79

Year	Revenue Expenditure (Cr)	Capital Expenditure (Cr)	Inc. Over Last Year
1999-00	35861.08	12616.47	10.91
2000-01	39668.78	14765.25	
2001-02	40029.29	16942.6	
2002-03	41072.16	14896.87	
2003-04	43376.2	16896.02	
2004-05	44833.16	32132.67	
2005-06			
2006-07	51517.04	34380.6	
2007-08	54773.27	37672.4	
2008-09	73578.66	40967.04	
2009-10	86879	54,824	
2010-11	87377	60,000	
2011-12	95,216.68	69198.81	
2012-13	113828.66	79578.63	

Source: Defence Service Estimate, Annual Reports Annual Reports, MoD

*Figures of some of the year is not available in the archives and other place

Chapter 5

India's Defence Modernization Program and the Issues of Procurement

Geographically and strategically India is positioned as an important setting that accentuates its strategic vulnerability as also provides lead-ins for playing a more dominant and pro-active role in the region. To ward off imminent threats and play a power role proportional to its size and potential, India needs continuing bolstering of several elements of its state power – economic, military, technological, international leverages etc. In this pecking order, acquiring sincere military deterrence and capabilities to inflict unaffordable losses on the adversaries will be critical.

India having the world's fourth largest force does not mean that it has adequate capability to deter, defeat and degrade external enemies or tackle externally geared up violent groups threatening internal security.[1] Defence capability of a nation requires host of other ingredients like qualitative and quantitative superiority in weapons and equipment, leadership and high moral of the fighting forces, intelligence capabilities, a reliable defence industrial infrastructure etc.

---

1. The Economist, (March 2013), "India as a great power Know your own strength" http://www.economist.com/news/briefing/21574458-india-poised-become-one-four-largest-military-powers-world-end. (Accessed in April 2013)

It is undeniably a disappointing fact that even after 64 years of independence one of the highest user of defence equipment, a country having the world's third largest pool of technical manpower and scientific talent and with a record of indigenously excelling in technologies of space, nuclear, information technology etc., is still dependent on foreign sources to meet 70% of its defence requirements.

As strategic analyst Brahma Chellaney rightly observes, India "invests bulk of its defence modernization resources not on strengthening its own armament base or deterrent capabilities but on promoting the military industry complex (MIC) of others."[2] Relying on large scale imports to equip the defence forces influences against our larger national interests as many of the imported items are not suitable for operation under Indian climate and environmental conditions, their costs are exorbitant, continuity of supply and renewal of spares is prone to political whims.

It must be highlighted that historically, the first ten years of post-independence were wasted in the area of defence production and developing R&D facilities, and no new ordnance factory was established leading to stagnation. Completely neglecting, either indigenous defence production or importing arms and equipment to keep the army in high state of defence preparedness.

However, following the 1962 Indo China war, the wisdom of expanding our defence production sector was realised, albeit at a heavy cost. New ideas were conceived and in course of time a number of new establishments and expansion of some existing units were undertaken. These corporations, commonly known as Defence Public Sector Unit (DPSU), gave a quantum jump to India's defence industry. Though they contribute substantially,

2. Ajit Doval, (Feb2012), "India's Defence Production and Research – Need for Transformational up-gradation", http://www.vifindia.org/article/2012/february/06/India-s-Defence-Production-and-Research-Need-for-Transformational-up-gradation. (Accessed in Feb2012)

their overall activities and up-gradation capabilities has left large areas uncovered.[3]

In the post 1962 when most of the European countries like Britain, France and Sweden and also US in the west refused to come forward and develop defence production relation with India, this led to the entry of the Soviet Union as a major supplier of defence equipment to India and, till today their share is estimated to be over 70%.[4] But the licensing system with USSR also tied India to production stereotypes, thwarting India's indigenous growth and innovativeness to develop high-end weapon systems from design to production stage.

Procurements and Its Issues

To keep our nation secure and dealing with threats to our national interests should be a priority for the Government. Without national security we cannot thrive as a nation. It is the bedrock on which all other achievements depend, whether stimulating renewed economic growth, improving public services or making the country a centre for innovation and enterprise. To keep the country secure we must provide our Armed Forces with the equipment and capabilities they need to operate in a rapidly changing security environment. Without the right equipment, delivered on time and where they need it, our Armed Forces simply cannot function and our national interests are put at risk. Effective procurement and support of defence equipment is therefore not a "nice to have", but an essential part of maintaining flexible, battle-winning Armed Forces.[5]

The global economic situation means that nearly all countries are faced with the need to limit public spending. Limited funds must be focused on where they will deliver most benefit, and we must make best use of the expertise available, whether it is in the private or public sector, to ensure that value for money for the

---

3. Athawale. S. Sanhita (2004), "Defence Services", New Delhi, Anmol Publications Pvt. Ltd.
4. Ibid.
5. Revi, A.P, (2008), 'Revolution in military Logistics', New Delhi, Indian Defence Review.

taxpayer is achieved. Defence cannot be immune - like all areas of public expenditure it needs to play its part in reducing the deficit and balancing the nation's accounts.

To maintain our defence capabilities at this challenging time we need to look hard at how we carry out every aspect of our business to see if it can be improved. Every single penny we can save on support functions is money that can be spent on the front-line. For at least the last several years our defence equipment program has suffered from waste and cost overruns. Equipment has been delivered late and to a specification that has not always met the requirements of our Armed Forces.[6]

The defence procurement and acquisition procedure is a complex and intricate process which needs to meet the twin objectives of modernization of the Armed Forces within reasonable time frames while confronting to the highest standards of transparency, probity and public accountability. The Defence Procurement Procedure is laid down for the assistance of the armed forces to ensure smooth acquisition of the weapons.

Chart 20 Ministry of Defence Structure (Transfer of technology)

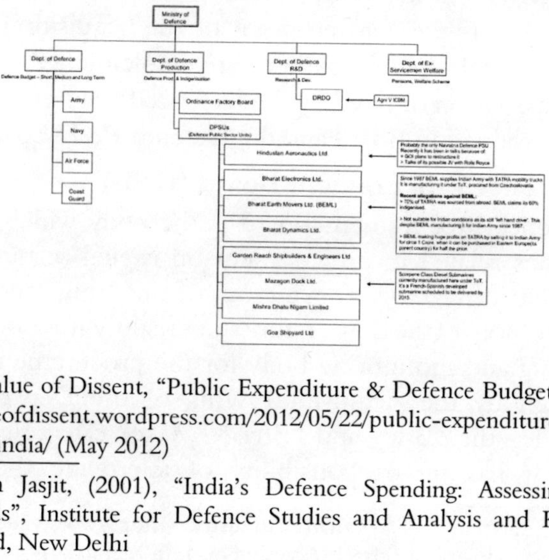

Source: Value of Dissent, "Public Expenditure & Defence Budget of India". http://valueofdissent.wordpress.com/2012/05/22/public-expenditure-defence-budget-in-india/ (May 2012)

6. Singh Jasjit, (2001), "India's Defence Spending: Assessing Future Needs", Institute for Defence Studies and Analysis and Knowledge World, New Delhi

The defence procurement procedures, method and its shortcomings

In 2001 the Ministry of Defence came out with the notification setting up the Defence Procurement Organization. The Defence Acquisition Council (DAC), headed by the Raksha Mantri was constituted under this new organization.

The defence procurement is a part of the wide organization called the Defence Procurement Organization which constitute of four major bodies which together play role in the procurement.[7] These bodies are as follows:

1. Defence Acquisition Council (DAC)

Defence Acquisition Council was constituted in August, 2001. DAC is the highest body headed by the Raksha Mantri (Defence Minister) which oversees the entire acquisition process for the Armed Forces. It approves the long-term perspective plans and accords the acceptance of necessity in each case of capital acquisition. This process of according the Acceptance of Necessity (AON) involves categorization of items into "Buy", "Buy & Make" and "Make". This process of approving the categorization is the starting point of the acquisition process. Decisions that follow from here are implemented under the overall supervision of DAC by the Defence Procurement Board, Defence Production Board and the Defence R&D Board.

2. Defence Procurement Board (DPB)

The Defence Procurement Board is the body which oversees all activities related to procurement on capital account in the Department of Defence flowing out of the "Buy" and "Buy & Make" decisions of the DAC. It functions mainly as a coordinating, supervising and monitoring body for the procurement process undertaken by the Acquisition Wing of the Department of Defence for the "Buy" and "Buy & Make" categories. In this process, it has the responsibility of approving the Annual

7. Confederation of Indian Industry, http://www.ciidefence.com/defenceindustry.asp?id=1, (Accessed on 15th March 2014)

Acquisitions Plans for the three Services. It essentially accords approvals to all major projects which are beyond the powers of the Raksha Mantri and require the approval of CCS or the Minister of Defence and Minister of Finance. Its functioning is governed by the Defence Procurement Procedure (DPP), which was modified in the year 2006. The Defence Secretary is the Chairman of this Board. Its Members include representatives from the various Departments in the Ministry of Defence, the three Wings of the Armed Forces, Chief of Integrated Defence Staff and the Member Secretary is the Financial Advisor in the Acquisition Wing of the Department of Defence.

3. Defence Production Board

Defence Production Board is a body, which is tasked to oversee indigenous manufacture and it derives its powers from the direction given by the DAC in respect of the categories of "Make" and "Buy & Make". It is expected to closely monitor the "make" projects, advise the DAC on policy issues regarding licensed production, ToT and new development projects. Its membership is very similar to the Defence Procurement Board with the exception that the Chairman OFB and some CMDs of the DPSUs are also included. The Member Secretary of the Defence Production Board is the Director, Planning & Coordination, in the Department of Defence Production.

4. Defence R&D Board

The Defence R&D Board has been constituted essentially to monitor and report on indigenous R&D proposals flowing out of the "Buy & make" and "Make" decisions of the DAC. It is a body that is expected to work closely with the Defence Production Board and to ensure that the transfer of technology from the laboratory to the factory is done in the most effective manner. The Chairman of this Board is the Scientific Advisor to RM and Secretary, R&D. Its Members are similar to the other two Boards with the exception that certain distinguished scientists have been included. The Member Secretary of this Board is the Chief Coordinator, R&D, in the DRDO Headquarters.

The Acquisition Wing of Department of Defence

The Acquisition Wing of the Department of Defence is the main secretariat that provides the necessary inputs to the Defence Procurement Board. This wing is headed by an officer of the rank of Special Secretary or Additional Secretary and is assisted by Financial Adviser (Acquisition) in the rank of Addl. Secretary and three Acquisition Managers, three Technical Managers and three Financial Managers, dealing with Land systems, Air and Maritime & Systems respectively, all in the rank of Joint Secretary.

The Acquisition Wing essentially deals with cases, which have been categorized as "Buy" or "Buy & Make". The guiding principles of procurement through the Acquisition Wing are contained in the notified Defence Procurement Procedure 2006.

Current Acquisition Practices

Presently Acquisition in MOD can be clearly demarcated into two separate sections. Firstly, the proposals being dealt with by the Acquisition Wing of the MOD, which is essentially functioning as a Procurement (Buying) Agency of MOD and therefore deals only with "Buy" and "Buy & Make" category of items. The second section is dealing with the "Make" category, which is essentially an acquisition process, akin to the acquisition procedure followed in major weapon producing countries.

The Defence Procurement Procedure (DPP)

It has been the constant endeavour of the Ministry of Defence, Government of India to introduce increased levels of transparency and accountability in the Defence Acquisition process. In this effort, the first step was the Defence Procurement Procedure - 2005, which has now been reviewed and revised in the year 2013. In addition, most importantly, a procedure for the development of systems based on indigenous research and design, categorized as 'MAKE', has now been formulated. This bridges a critical gap that existed hitherto, and would provide the requisite framework for increased participation of Indian industries.

In the year 2006 the Kelkar Committee redefined the terms "Buy", "Buy & make" and "Make".

According to it the revised definition in para 4 of DPP are as under:-

Acquisition Covered under the "Buy" Decision: Buy would mean an outright purchase of equipment. Based on the sources of procurement, this category would be classified as "Buy (Indian)" and "Buy (Global)". "Buy (Indian)" would mean India vendors only and "Global" would foreign as well as Indian vendors. "Buy Indian" must have at least and minimum of 30% of indigenous content if the systems are being integrated by an Indian vendor.

Acquisition covered under the "Buy & Make" decision would mean purchase from foreign vendor followed by licensed production/ indigenous manufacture in the country.

Acquisitions covered under "Make" decision would include high technology complex systems to be designed, developed and produced indigenously.

Some of the important features of Defence Procurement Procedure - 2013 include:[8]

1. The first major change that has been brought in relates to the introduction of the 'preferred categorisation' in the following order; Buy (Indian), Buy & Make (Indian), Make (Indian), Buy & Make, Buy (Global). While seeking the approval for Accord of Necessity (AoN) in a particular category, say, Buy (Global), it will now be necessary to give justification for not considering the other higher preference categories. This is expected to give a stronger impetus to indigenization.

8. Salient Features of Defence Procurement Procedure- 2013 (June 2013) http://pib.nic.in/newsite/erelease.aspx?relid=96361 (Accessed on July 2013)

2. Stipulations related to the indigenous content have been clarified and made more stringent. Indigenous content requirements will now extend all the way to the lowest tier of the sub-vendor. Hence, import content in the products supplied by the sub-vendors will not qualify towards indigenous content.
3. Besides this, the requirement of the prescribed indigenous content, e.g. 30% in the Buy (Indian) category is to be achieved on the overall cost basis, as well as in the core components i.e. the basic equipment, manufacturers recommended spares, special tools and test equipments taken together. In addition, the basic equipment must also have minimum 30% indigenous content at all stages including the one offered at the trial stage. It has further been stipulated that an indigenization plan will be provided by the vendor. These stipulations will ensure more meaningful efforts towards indigenization.
4. While a penalty has been stipulated for not achieving the required indigenous content at a given stage, a scope to make up the deficiency at later stages has been provided.
5. Likewise, in the Buy and Make (Indian) cases, there is no stipulation regarding the minimum indigenous content in the Buy component and the Indian vendor is given the elbow room to achieve the prescribed indigenous content in the overall delivery. This enables the Indian vendor the time to absorb Transfer of Technology (ToT) and, set up manufacturing facility while concurrently meeting the service requirements.
6. A method for assessment of indigenous content, based on self certification by vendors, has been given while keeping provision for audit by MoD or its nominated agency, if found necessary.
7. A major set of changes aimed at making the procurement process speedier includes the stipulation to finalize the SQRs before seeking the accord for 'Acceptance of Necessity' and reducing the validity period of an AoN from

2 years to one year. This will bring down the processing time of individual cases significantly.

8. Procurement cases are also expected to be speeded up on account of enhanced delegation of powers of the SCAPCHC from Rs 50 Crores to 150 Crores and the power of the DPB from 150 crores to 300 crores.
9. In order to encourage timely submission of the bids by the vendors and to discourage last minute requests for extension of time, it has been stipulated that any request for extension of the bid submission date must be made at least two weeks prior to the bid submission date with adequate justification.
10. Impetus to indigenization would also require simplification of the Buy and Make (Indian) and Make procedure. The exercise to simplify the Buy and Make (Indian) procedure has been completed doing away inter alia with the requirement of short-listing the vendors through the 'Project Appraisal Committee' while keeping the validity of the AoN to two years permitting comprehensive consultations with the Industry. This is expected to bring more projects under the Buy and Make (Indian) category. Simplification of the Make procedure is underway and is expected to be completed in few months.
11. In Buy (Global) cases, it will now be possible for the Indian vendor to give Maintenance ToT to another Indian vendor of their choice. The Maintenance ToT partners no longer required to be nominated by the DDP.
12. The appendix F and G to the RFP i.e. the Payment Terms and Commercial Offer have been recast as 'Commercial Clauses' and 'Evaluation Criteria of Price Bid Format'. These include use of the International Commercial Terms (INCOTERMS 2010), bringing payment terms for Indian Bidders on par with those for the foreign bidders, specificity in stages and modes of payment and removal of excise duty in determination of L-1.

Apart from the major salient features of the DPP 2013 enumerated above, a number of other changes have been made which are procedural in nature and aim at bringing clarity and efficiency and in the procurement procedures. Further measures to strengthen the Indian Defence Sector are under consideration and will be brought about after due consultation with all stake holders. In the meantime, it is expected that this document will be well received by the Industry, the users and other stakeholders at large in the Indian Defence Sector.

The starting point of a procurement proposal is the Statement of Case (SoC) prepared by the Service Headquarter (SHQ) concerned. The SoC is then sent for comments to the officers concerned in the Administrative Branch of the Department of Defence (DoD), Department of Defence Production (DDP), Defence Research & Development Organization (DRDO) and the finance division of the MoD.

The flow chart explains the procurement procedure:

Chart 21: Procurement Procedure

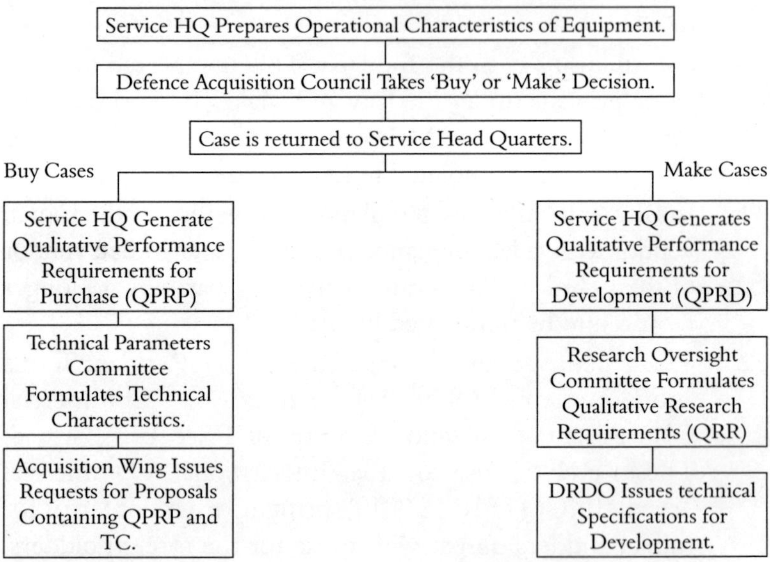

Source: United Service Institute, DSSC Pre Staff material

After going throw the flow chart we need to understand where the problem lies and causes delays and failures of procurement to reach its final stage and acquisition afterwards.

Causes for Delay

Divergent Views Causing Confusion

It is usually said that in a group effort the results are always good and the more the idea the better the results. However in the case of defence procurement, 'more the merrier' formula cannot be applied.

The divergence of views on the proposed categorization could also appear in the Services Capital Acquisition Pan Categorization Committee (SCAPCC), Service Capital Acquisition Plan Higher Categorization Committee (SCAPCHC) and Defence Procurement Board (DPB)/ Defence Acquisition Council (DAC) through which every procurement proposal must travel before it is accorded Acceptance of Necessity (AoN), which is nothing but approval-in-principle to commence the tendering process.

Considering that all these committees in the chain of decision making have members from the DoD, DDP, DRDO, Finance Division and, last but not the least, the services, divergence of views on issues, including the proposed categorization, could result in processing of the proposal taking longer than what it would take if every aspect of the proposal is in accordance with some laid down guidelines.[9]

Issue of Categorization

The issue of categorization has been a major factor contributing to protracted deliberations over a procurement proposal. In order to categorize the equipment as "Buy", "Buy & Make" and "Make" the proposal runs into a difficulty as there are no guidelines that could be followed to nominate the Indian

9. United Service Institute, DSSC Pre Staff material

companies from the private sector to whom the Request for Proposal (RFP) or guidelines to nominate an Indian Production Partner (IPP).

An Ambitious Equipment Program

This can be exacerbated by the very natural ambition throughout MOD to maximize the level of capability that can be achieved from the resources available, and a historic reluctance to make painful choices to balance budgets. Too broad a range of tasks and too many types of equipment being ordered (sometimes at too high a specification) has led to a situation where all too often the list of planned requirements has significantly exceeded the funding available to pay for them. This behaviour has been reinforced by a "conspiracy of optimism", between military specifies and industrial partners, systematically underestimating the costs (and delivery times) of new projects.

Historically, this has resulted in an equipment program that is overheated: and that in turn has led to an annual consideration of what should be delayed or deferred in order to balance the budget that year. These delays themselves often carry significant financial implications, known as "frictional costs".

An unstable interface between the Requester and Deliverer

At present, the interface between the DE&S and the rest of the MOD (including the three Service headquarters, known as the Front Line Commands) is porous. The moral imperative to ensure that our servicemen have the best possible equipment and support has given rise to a tendency to agree to changes requested at any point in the program without a full understanding of the consequences of these changes. For example – the Requester may ask for changes to be made to the specification of a particular piece of equipment late in its development, when incorporating those changes would delay the in-service date by years, and make it considerably more expensive. If the Requester had been better able to understand the implications of making that change, he may have chosen to retain the original specification.

This behaviour is in part the result of a situation in which individuals in both military and civilian, can feel unable to express and maintain an independent position, perhaps for reasons of hierarchical pressure, even when they believe that it is supported by robust analysis. It is exacerbated when demands to incorporate changes over short timescales make accurate cost and time estimating difficult. Over time, this "can do" attitude in fact harms the Armed Forces by driving an unsustainable program, necessitating deep cuts to make savings when a more effective, disciplined control of the program could have made better use of tax payers money and resulted in increased operational output.[10]

(United Service Institute, DSSC Pre Staff material)

Insufficient Skills and Management Freedoms Within the system

The skills and expertise which DPA needs to perform its role effectively are very different to those required and valued by much of the rest of the Civil Service. It requires a high proportion of Project Management, Commercial and Financial experts as well as engineers and other technical specialists. It needs this expertise to discharge its responsibility for delivering a project portfolio that is amongst the most complex in the world. These specialist skills have a much higher market value than can be recognized within the civil service pay framework. Whilst many civilian staff in DPA have wider motivations than simply the size of their salaries, for example the interest and variety of the work on offer, and the satisfaction of supporting our Armed Forces, it is becoming increasingly difficult to recruit, develop, and retain those with the particular skills needed at all levels.

Unrealistic General Service Qualitative Requirements (GSQR)

The principal cause for delay in the procurement of Military Equipments has been the unrealistic formation of General

10. United Service Institute, DSSC Pre Staff material

Services Qualitative Requirements (SQR). It refers to essential characteristics of proposed military equipments projected against a specific time period to counter an estimated enemy threat or to fill other operational needs. GSQR is really a basic building block on which the complete edifice of procurement system is based. The entire procurement process is, therefore, directed towards getting the equipment, which satisfies the laid down SQRs. Deviations to SQRs can only be sanctioned by the defence Minister on the recommendations of the Defence Procurement Board (DPB) and is a highly complex and time consuming process.

Reasons for the unrealistic GSQRs

The task of preparing the first draft is assigned to the concerned branch where all available books are collected and best characteristics of all known equipment are complied as essential requirements. As the draft of SQR travels upwards in official hierarchy it gathers more parameters and there are no deletions, thus, the final SQR takes the shape of a well complied 'wish list' of utopian dimensions.

SQRs are made without the services without considering the technologies available or likely to be available in the planed time frame and no inputs are obtained from the industry as regards their capability. SQRs are the same whether the equipment is to be purchased outright or developed indigenously forcing development agencies to embark upon new and unknown technologies which are highly expensive, time consuming and an uncertain exercise.

Also another important flaw is that the parameters are too general in nature, vague, unverifiable and cannot be quantified at all. For example: vehicle needs to be compact, strong, sturdy and with excellent running characteristics.

Most importantly all the three services of the armed forces work in a watertight compartment. The officers are not given the opportunity and authority to think out of the box and power to go beyond the said guidelines. Due to several limitations, like the money, time, hierarchy and the traditional working patterns.

The Will to do it

Now coming to the final point of the failures in successful procurement procedure, is the will power to do the job in time and in a successful and most rational way. The officers who are elected to do this job are most of the time not serious about the task in hand. They do not put in the innovative idea and realistic approach to the brain storming session and come out with some unrealistic SQR. The groups of officers sometimes don't come from technical background and so they fail to understand the technical aspect of the requirement to be projected. Mostly it is a copy paste job that leads to break in the working procedure.

Once the paper is forward in the higher offices they do not bother to look into the paper as their mind is already pre occupied. Sometimes the personal interest of the officers also comes in way of the smooth functioning of the procurement procedure. The motivation to do work honestly and dedication amongst the official is dying its slow death.

While adequate provisions exist in the manuals for services and the guidelines for procurement and to address issues relating to sustenance and adequate linkages exist between acquisition and sustenance. However, they are not fully implemented and integrated nor they are completely read and understood by the officials.

Moreover, the bureaucratic delays in decision making, personal interest, no drive to do things innovatively instead accepting everything said by the seniors, the extremely hierarchical system are some of the reasons for further delays in procurement and ultimately rollover of the defence budget for the financial year of the same.

Suggestions and Conclusion

The government has professed its inclination to promote indigenous production of defence products over and over again but unfortunately something seems to be holding the ministry back in taking on the issue wholeheartedly. In order to go full steam on the bandwagon of indigenization the following is recommended:

The Services headquarters should prepare and forward only Operational Characteristics of the equipment sought, i.e. military characteristics pertaining primarily to the functions to be performed by the equipment either together with it or in conjunction with other equipment.

Defence Acquisition Council (DAC) under Defence Ministry should deliberate upon the case to decide on make' or 'buy' approach and then the case be returned to service HQ to Qualitative Performance Requirements for Purchase (QPRP) for 'buy' cases and Qualitative Performance Requirements for Development (QPRD) for 'make' cases respectively.

SQRs for equipment to be procured should be based on the equipment in production in the world market while SQRs for indigenous development should be based on the current level of technology, research proficiency and the time frame assigned.

The SQRs should always be realistic, broad based and spelt out in terms of verifiable functional characteristics.

Explore very possibility of manufacturing the item required in India, even if it means only assembling SKDs with very minimal value addition by a local industry. The idea being that even such assembling is going to bring some better knowledge and understanding for the industry and their trained manpower in India. Progressively increasing the value addition being done by the local industry should be rewarded through a scheme of incentives. No price preference should be given.

The method of setting up manufacturing in India could be through establishment of JV, collaborative arrangements or even by purchase of technology by the industry. Government should not make exclusively direct payment for technology, but instead encourage the industry to take initiative and workout arrangements so that this cost of technology is merged in the cost of the manufactured item and the industry which is able to reduce production ost through increased efficiency and use of local material is advantaged.

The government should come up with incentive scheme which encourages easy transfer of technology from foreign sources and manufacture in the country. The scheme should contain provisions for higher incentives for greater value additions by local industry and also transfer of critical technologies.

Only when there is no possibility of manufacturing in the country at more economical prices should the MoD resort to direct purchase from foreign sources.

There may be a few cases where the item listed in the Long Term Integrated Perspective Plan (LTIPP) is manufactured only by one industry in the world. In such cases the MoD should adopt an approach similar to the Foreign Military Sales (FMS) in USA, or a direct government to government negotiation. Further in such cases if MoD desires to have licensed production in the country following purchase of fully formed items they should follow the procedure presently being used for "Buy and Make" items.

Creating a new Government-Owned Contractor Operated (GOCO) operating model to manage the procurement and support of defence equipment by the Defence Equipment and Support organization as the Agent of the MOD, subject Better Defence Acquisition: Improving how we procure and support Defence equipment to demonstrating affordability and value for money. This will bring in incentivized private sector expertise to improve the delivery of the MOD's equipment program by introducing systems and ways of working that provide staff with the best access to the necessary skills, processes and tools to enable them to do their jobs better, driving value for money in equipment projects.

Creating, a new statutory framework to ensure transparency and to encourage efficiency in single-source procurement contracts. This will provide an assurance that value for money is being obtained for the taxpayer in this significant area of MOD. The changes will be real and long lasting, underpinned by legislation where required. I hope these changes will enjoy widespread support. They are the right thing to do and now it is the right time to do them.

Offset Policy

Another important factor in the procurement policy is the offset policy which we have discussed superficially in the Para's above. But as it is a significant topic we need to deliberate little further in order to understand its role.

First and foremost readers should understand the meaning of the term offset. According to my understanding of offset it is "An agreement between two parties whereby a supplier agrees to buy products from the party to whom it is selling, in order to win the buyer as a customer and offset buyer's outlay." Generally the seller is the foreign company and buyer is a government that stipulates that the seller must then agree to buy products from companies within their country. These agreements are the legal trade practices in the defence industry. In other words some would even call it some sort of barter.

In India, offsets were introduced in the year 2005 towards strengthening self- reliance in Defence Preparedness, but objectives were not available in any public document. The offset provisions were elaborated in DPP 2006. Banking of offset was introduced in DPP 2008. These objectives were made available for the first time issued in August 2012 as an amendment to DPP 2011.

The key objective of Indian Defence Offset Policy is to leverage capital acquisitions to develop Indian defence industry by (i) fostering development of internationally competitive enterprises,

(ii) augmenting capacity for Research, Design, and Development related to defence products and services and (iii) encouraging development of synergetic sectors like civil aerospace, and internal security.

The procedure for offset implementation is given at Appendix D and relevant annexure to Chapter I of DPP 2013. The technical details of offset obligations means the details of products, the Indian Offset Partners (IOP) and the amount phases and the time plan. The vendors, prior to the plan for participating in the procurement project need to have this tie up firmly committed or atleast have the papers stating that IOP tie up has been carried out.

The avenue for discharge of offset obligation is the second area which needs to be considered as per Sub Para 3.1 in case the vendor is eligible for multiplier effect, the same also needs to be mentioned upfront. The time frame and the offset being part of the main project or otherwise also needs to be mentioned. The list of Tier I sub contractors are another area where the vendors falter.

Proposals for technology acquisition, provision of equipment and/or Transfer of Technology (TOT) to Government institutions and establishments engaged in the manufacture and or maintenance of eligible products and provision of eligible services including DRDO. This will include augmenting capacity for research, design, development, training and education but excludes civil infrastructure multipliers.

The latest policy has encouraged technology absorption by DRDO through the route of offsets. Acquisition of technology will be developed by DRDO. The government has now facilitated DRDO in technology acquisition through the offset route for critical technologies. The acquisition of technology by DRDO can certainly help it to take a leap on to next level and sustain developments thereafter.

However there seems to be no end to the growing problems for the offset policy even after more than a year of its release last year. These problems have arisen primarily because the Defence Offset Management Wing (DOMW) set up with the aim to manoeuvre the offset policy continues to be perceived as the preserve of the Acquisition Wing. This is like history repeating itself with DOMW going the same way as the earlier avatar Defence Offset Facilitation Agency (DOFA). DOMW was created precisely because of the realization that DOFA had not been able to meet the requirements. The present lethargy is due to the division of responsibility between the Acquisition Wing and the DOMW and the latter not being empowered to discharge the functions assigned to it.[11]

The Acquisition Wing is responsible for technical and commercial evaluation of offset proposals received in response to the Request for Proposal (RFP) and conclusion of offset contracts. The DOMWs responsibility include (a) formulation of defence offset guidelines, (b) monitoring the discharge of offset obligations, including audit and review of progress reports received from the vendors, (c) participation in technical and commercial evaluation of offset proposals as members of the Technical Offset Evaluation Committee (TOEC) and Contract Negotiate Committee (CNC) (d) administration of penalties under offset contracts in consultation with the Acquisition Wing. (e) Assisting vendors in interfacing with the Indian industry.[12]

Criticism

Though the division of power between the Acquisition Wing and the DOMW has eased out certain procedure there still continues to be some areas of concern. Several problems are inherent in this division of responsibility, beginning with the responsibility for formulation of the offset guidelines. It is no secret that the 2012 policy was the initiative taken by the Acquisition Wing.

11. Iyer MKK, (2014),'Musings of a Serving Army Officer: The Indian Offset Policy', Global Defence Offset Review, New Delhi
12. Cowshish Amit, (2014), 'Indian Defence Offset Policy: Need to break out of inertia', Global Defence Offset Review ', New Delhi

The policies promulgated then are comprehensive and there is no need for the reformulation of the same. However what is desirable at this stage is to make some improvements in policies such as empowering the MoD to channelize the offsets into specific areas rather than leaving it to the vendors to decide how they want to discharge their obligations. The issue is that in this case the DOMW should take the lead because as per the formal division this task is not under the Acquisition Wing. Therefore, by default the DOMW should show interest and initiate the interactions with the industries and overcome piddle issues in consultation with other ministries and departments of the government. There is also need to organize a forum for the interaction between the MoD and the industries on a regular interval bases.

The second problem is the evaluation of the offset proposals and conclusion of the offset contract. This responsibility has been cast on the Acquisition Wing but this duty cannot be performed without the equal participation from DOMW in the Technical Offset Evaluation Committee (TOEC) and the Contract Negotiate Committee (CNC).

The Acquisition Wing is under the administrative control of the Department of Defence and the DOMW is administered by the Department of Defence Production (DPP). This gives rise to lack of coordination and communication leading to delay in decision making. Another fact for this kind of delay is that the DOMW is not equipped with the skills required for making meaningful contribution in the deliberation of TOEC and the CNC which was the same problem with the DOFA. The important point to observe here is that have we learnt anything from our past failures or is it like "old wine in new bottle"?

The third problem is arising from this division of responsibility is related to providing the interface between the vendors and the Indian industry. For one thing, it is not clear what does it mean and for another it is open to question whether DOMW is equipped to handle this task. It is very unlikely that DOMW could provide this interface, given the basic instinct of every government official not to be seen in getting involved in such an affair.

However, the guidelines despite several amendments in the DPP, latest being 2013, have not been successful in expediting arms acquisition. There have been numerous cases where crucial acquisition proposals have been cancelled midways and retendered thereafter, with some having witnessed the process being repeated several times without success. Asa consequences, the MoD had to surrender year after year huge amount of its procurement budget and more importantly the country's defence preparedness has remained at a below desired level.[13]

As has been reported by various agencies like the Comptroller and Auditor General of India and the Parliamentary Standing Committee on Defence, in terms of the armed forces with equipment and support services, has been at a sub-optimum level. The Army, for example, is short of even some basic items such as bullet proof jackets and night vision devices. Moreover, it has not been able to procure a single artillery gun since the Bofors guns were last inducted. The Air Force, which operates a lesser number of aircraft then officially mandated, is also short of radars for its surveillance and counter measures. The Navy, whose warship strength is less than the sanctioned level, is facing a severe crisis in its most potent force multipliers: submarines.

Recommendations

Some bold steps are required to be taken to get out of this indolence. Such as:[14]

First step should be to that the MoD can engage a consultant to work on issues related to refinement of the 2012 policy and providing clarifications on numerous doubts which have been

13. Ibid.
14. Iyer MKK, (2014),'Musings of a Serving Army Officer: The Indian Offset Policy', Global Defence Offset Review, New Delhi

raised. Based on the suggestions provided through consultation by varied ministries, department and stake holders, the consultant can prepare a comprehensive proposal for approval from the Defence Acquisition Council. And later the decisions should be posted on the DOMW website. This will provide much needed transparency clarity to the industry or suppliers.

Secondly, the present policy permits DOMW to take the assistance of any appropriate entry to discharge its functions. As an extension of this principle, MoD needs to seriously consider an alternative to DOMW itself for such functions as monitoring the offset contracts, carrying out audit and processing of the proposals for banking of offset credits. These functions can be performed better by an entity which has a greater permanency and can build institutional memory and competence. Such an agency could be created as a part of the Defence Accounts Department and serve as the secretariat for the decision making authorities in the MoD.

Thirdly the outside support to the TOEC and CNC by DOMW should give way to officials well versed in matters related to offset being made an integral part of these committees, just as the finance members are the integral part of the CNCs. This will make the Acquisition Wing entirely responsible for the conclusion of the offset contracts.

Fourthly, the task of providing an interface between the vendors and the Indian industry should be left to the industry itself. To make such interface more focused, the defence industry could consider creating a defence- specific forum.

Although the DPP stipulates time frame for each of the stage of procurement, it is often not adhered to due to various reasons, the vital being the absence of a strong monitoring system, lack of professionalism among the acquisition functionaries and short tenure posting of the personnel involved.

To rectify the shortcomings the supreme auditor had recommended the following:

An integrated defence acquisition organization can be considered by incorporating all the functional elements and specialization involved in defence acquisition under one roof. This should be accompanied by adequate re-formulation of the whole process of acquisition to identify and remove the redundant activities.

A specialized cadre/pool of Acquisition managers may be developed by imparting suitable training in different areas of acquisition viz. project management, contract negotiations and management and exposure to professional best practices of procurement. Certain stability of tenure of the personnel should also be ensured.

A suitable integrated electronic information system connecting all defence procurement should be put in place to support the acquisition process.

These recommendation were passed around ten to eleven years have been passed. Bearing in mind that these acquisitions involves enormous amount of wealth that is coming from the common mans tax payment, the Ministry of Defence should come out of its cocoon and implement the aforesaid implementations at the earliest without further ado.

If the above said suggestions can be implemented to the present offset policy we can hope to have a smooth functioning system. However the mantra to be reminded again and again is that time seems to be running out.

Chapter 6

Conclusion

People will spend to defend what they consider important enough to defend and are normally willing to pay the price they consider necessary. But we have not clearly articulated our strategic doctrine so far. The estimates committee of the parliament had expressed its unhappiness at the absence of a clearly spelt out doctrine for India's defence.

In the absence of a well established doctrine, there is a strong tendency to simply keep on building on the existing force levels and structures in what can only be described as an add on strategy. Lack of articulation of the strategic doctrine operates against the building and sustaining of a national consensus on defence policies.[1] India's primary strategic objective, of necessity must continuously seek durable peace and security so that socioeconomic growth and development can be pursued without adverse impulses. Thus deterrence should be a central factor in the doctrine while détente and strategic stability to be pursued vigorously in a sustained way.

Our problem is that resource assessment beyond the current year is rarely carried out in defence planning. Even this is undertaken in the last days of the financial closing and we happily accept the concept that defence could be given more funds above the budget "if required".

---

1. Karnad Bharat, (2005) 'India's Future Plans and Defence Requirements', "Emerging India: Security and Foreign Policy Perspectives" ed., New Delhi, Institute for Defence Studies and Analysis and Promilla & Co., Publishers

The Five Year defence plans have lost their utility for resource planning. In reality, resource allocation is a government function and cannot be undertaken by the service headquarters without the government indicating the basis of what might be available.[2] This factor alones requires that a strategic planning division be set up in the Ministry of Defence to undertake the task of long term defence planning in a coherent manner linked to resource availability and which commits the requisite resources after examining alternative choices of policy and their costs.

India exhibits a striking lack of what might be called a strategic culture. Yet its political class shows little sign of knowing or caring how the country's military clout should be deployed.

It is true that defence must be need based and cannot be pegged to arbitrary benchmarks, but barring dramatic changes like the conduct of a war, defence policies also remain evolutionary. Thus the past data can be very valuable in assessment of future needs. From this can evolve the planning parameters for resource availability and commitment for the years ahead. In fact we need to shift from threat based to capability based defence planning.

Military Equipment and Life Cycle

Military equipment normally has a technical design life closer to 20 years and the operational life normally averages around a similar period. Technological progress, in fact, is tending to stretch the technical life of equipment closer to 30 years now.[3] Department of Defence (DoD) military equipment continues to experience increasedusage and fatigue due to combat and contingency operations. Higher than expected utilizationrates and fatigue caused by operating environment and mission

2. Singh Jasjit, (2001), "India's Defence Spending: Assessing Future Needs", Institute for Defence Studies and Analysis and Knowledge World, New Delhi
3. Masters, Jonathan, (Nov 2011),'Defence Spending and Deficit Debate', Council on Foreign Relations, http://www.cfr.org/defense-budget/defense-spending-deficit-debate/p26442 (Accessed in January 2013)

requirements are resulting inreduced service life expectancies for some of the military equipment. This isleading to new and emerging requirements for capital planning and military equipment replacement and recapitalization.

'Life cycle concept' or also called as 'Womb to Tomb' view is not being taken for EM, which is a major cause of poor sustainment of existing capability particularly with regard to complex and advanced weapon systems viz, Tank T-72 and T-90 S, AD weapon systems, Schilka, OSA –AK, Fire support systems such as Smerch etc.[4]

Eventually measure of success lies in the functioning of the formulated strategy after the system has been deployed for operational exploitation, though acquisition phase activities are crucial to designing, developing and implementing a successful and affordable sustainment strategy. Therefore, a sustainment viewpoint cannot be predetermined and applicable to all equipment / class of equipment across the equipment profile. It needs to be practical, developing and in-sync with the operational and employment philosophies of equipment based on potential required from the weapon system that has to be inducted. Further it can be upgraded with latest technology/engine/ tools etc. once the equipment is obsolete post-induction, based on operational, technological and environmental factors.

The doctrine of Total Life Cycle System Management (TLCSM) and Performance Based Logistics (PBL) are very flexible tools which emphasise upon an early focus on sustainment within the system lifecycle.

TLCSM is the execution, supervision and oversight by the designated Program Manager (PM) of all activities associated with the acquisition development, production, fielding, sustainment and disposal of a weapon system across its lifecycle. It empowers

---

4. Hardy James,(October 2013), "India's Defence Procurement Bungles", The Diplomat, http://thediplomat.com/2013/10/indias-defense-procurement-bungles/?allpages=yes (Accessed in October 2013)

the PM as the lifecycle manager with complete responsibility for system acquisition and follow on sustainment.

It is thus apparent from the above evaluation that there is surely need for an all-inclusive analysis and reconsideration of the prevailing system for equipment sustainment to make it receptive to operational imperatives and to establish link between acquisition and sustenance.

Leveraging sustainment through acquisition by adopting a Total Life Cycle Costing (TLCC) approach coupled with PBL and exploiting the provisions of DPP towards sustenance will not only ensure 'bang for the buck' but also conserve capability.

To address these challenges, Department of Defence requires a standardized, repeatable, and supportable process to account for changes in Operational tempo (OPTEMPO) for the military equipment. This will assist with justifying budget requests for military equipment replacement and recapitalization, as well as capital planning.

Defence capability

India having the world's fourth largest fighting force does not imply that it has an adequate capability to deter, defeat and degrade its adversaries or tackle violent groups threatening the internal security of a nation. Defence capability of a nation requires lots of other components like qualitative and quantitative dominance in weapons and equipment, intelligence capabilities, leadership and high moral of the fighting forces, a reliable defence industrial infrastructure etc.

India inherited an undeveloped defence production infrastructure from the British at the time of attaining independence. The first ten years after independence were the washed out in the area of defence production and development of R&D facilities. No new ordnance factory was established or R&D capabilities developed which led to stagnation.

During the Nehruvian era, India developed no concept of forward strategic planning while expenditure on strengthening national security was seen as non-productive drain on scarce resources. Nehru thought that overall industrialisation of the country and establishing basic industries – the new temples of modern India - will automatically meet the defence requirements, a low priority item in his national agenda.

While self sufficiency was the belief of those times, the basic approach adopted was to develop self sufficiency in mainstream industries, completely neglecting either indigenous defence production or importing arms and equipment to keep the army updated and well equipped.

An important point that was completely ignored was the fact that defence production was a highly specialised sector requiring heavy investments, a strong Research & Development back up and production, from design to production and eventual integration, had a long development period and is not an overnight process.

With the Chinese threat looming in the Indian minds, the Defence Research and Development Organisation (DRDO) was created in 1958. But it was a half hearted exercise and the DRDO was starved of resources, quality technical manpower and lacked high level strategic path. Unwillingness of western countries to transfer defence technologies or agree to industrial collaboration clubbed with bureaucratic controls - bereft both of expertise and security sensitivity – created the problem of weak production house.

Indian scientist community should work on the line of developing the standard of air to surface warfare which had remained constrained to line of sight (LOS) operations. As compared to the world war era when the target was first identified and then the weapon was launched. As the aircrafts speeds increased with the jet age, this also meant very little time to undertake these tasks and specially with the moving targets like the tanks and vehicles. The programme should be developed compressing the sensor-to-shooter time from hours (that happened in earlier days) to few minutes which is the mantra of the day.

The concept "self-sufficiency" differs from "self-reliance" which is used alternative in the Indian defence preparedness context. Self-sufficiency means producing everything in house that the armed forces need, whereas self-reliance refers to "equipping the armed forces with whole range of equipments that may come from foreign and domestic sources". However, 'self-sufficiency' is not an ideal path for a country like India since India's industrial and Research and Development (R&D) base is not yet sufficiently developed.

Problem of unspent budget

India post independence adopted the budgeting system like so many other procedures and processes from the British. But the UK recognised the need to improve the system and process and changed its accounting and budgeting system for the defence forces. This had improved their decision making capability for cost effective utilisation of funds. However in India no such reviews and changes have taken place. As result the record has been unsatisfactory mostly because there had been no improvement.

Even as the threats and challenges to national security have sprouted in recent decades, the modernisation plans of the Armed Forces have been stagnating as large amounts of unspent funds on the capital account – meant for procurement – are surrendered each year. Bureaucratic red-tapism slows down the acquisition process and defence procurement is dependent almost entirely on imports as the Indian defence industry has not yet not developed fully and still depends on the external support. The defence procurement process has been backbreaking and overdue despite recent policy reforms and is only recently it began to come out of the quagmire that it was languishing in.

India's modernisation can at best be described as being undertaken in fits and starts, the present quantitative gap will soon become a qualitative gap as well. If the present slow pace process of modernisation is allowed to continue. By the end of India's 13th Defence Plan (2017-2022), China's militarily will become strong enough to force India to submit to the solution to the territorial and boundary dispute on China's whims and fancies. [5]

The request for allotment of funds projected by the three Services every year to the MoD is further projected by the MoD to the Ministry of Finance (MoF). The MoF treats the MoD's projections as a "wish list" and reduces them further by an average of almost 25 percent.[6] As an illustration, during 2004-05, the Services projected a requirement of approximately Rs 103,000 crore the MoD reduced it to about Rs 87,000 crore; and, the MoF allotted Rs 77,000 crore, a shortfall of 26 percent.[7] This reduction is effected without rhyme or reason and mostly without discussion with the Armed Forces so that almost till the day of the budget, the Services are uncertain of their likely budgetary allocation for the next financial year.

The Committee are deeply concerned to note that the Ministry of Defence was compelled to surrender funds of Rs. 5,000 crore Rs. 9,000 crore and Rs. 5,000 crore at the Revised Estimates stage of 2001-02, 2002-03 and 2003-04, respectively, to meet the deficits. The budgetary ceilings imposed by the Ministry of Finance in the year 2005-06 have led to the downsizing of the total projected capital requirements of the Defence Services from adequately Rs. 44123.86 crore to Rs. 34375.14 crore, which fails to address the security concerns of the nation.[8]

A large chunk of the funds earmarked for capital expenditure, which goes towards modernisation, is surrendered year after year. Successive Finance Ministers have been using reductions

---

5. KanwalGurmeet, (2010), 'Low Defence Budget hampering Modernisation Plans', India Strategic, http://www.indiastrategic.in/topstories546.htm
6. Ibid. P. 1
7. Ibid. P. 1
8. Ibid. P.. 2

in the defence budget at the Revised Estimates (RE) stage as one of the tools to manage the country's burgeoning fiscal deficit.

The Standing Committee on Defence has observed: "The Committee also observe that every year the annual budgetary allocation for the armed forces, particularly for capital acquisition, is being reduced at RE stage as a result of which a number of schemes do not fructify, which causes delay and cost overruns in the modernisation of the armed forces."[9]

Funds as well remain unspent due to bureaucratic red tape and the fear of strictures being passed by the Central Vigilance Commissioner for tardy defence procurement procedures.

The surrender of fund in the past few years has become a matter of serious concern. Surrender of funds year after year indicates improper planning and inability to meet the critical requirements of the services.

There are host of reasons for the surrender of the fund such as the bureaucratic delays; delays in conclusion of price negotiations with approved vendors, non-pursuing of the procurement cases with the desired earnestness, non release of stage payments from ministry on time.

In addition ministry of finance also indicates cuts in defence budget at times, at the end of the financial year, in order to address the more important problem of reducing fiscal deficit of the government.

Gradually declining defence budget in terms of constant rupees are slowly but surely eroding national security capabilities. Continuous deployment of the armed forces, particularly the Indian Army, for various operational commitments and the almost complete lack of genuine modernisation are undermining preparedness for war and eating into the slight qualitative edge that they have enjoyed over India's military adversaries.

---

9. KanwalGurmeet, (2010), 'Low Defence Budget hampering Modernisation Plans', India Strategic, http://www.indiastrategic.in/topstories546.htm

With the economy growing at the compound rate of seven to eight per cent annually, surely the nation can afford to invest 3.0 to 3.5 per cent of its GDP as an insurance premium for national security. The government of the day must show the concern and political courage essential to safeguard national security interests by making adequate financial provisions for the modernisation of the armed forces. The results of not doing so will be staggeringly atrocious.

Keeping in view the void in India's defence preparedness and rising military expenditure and capability in its neighbourhood, a small increase in the budget seems inadequate.

Considering the fact that India spends a moderate portion of its gross national output, there a scope of progressively enhancing defence allocation to at least 2.5 to 3 percent of GDP. However, the enhancement of allocation would largely be dependent on timely utilisation of such allocations. As the evidence shows, the MoD has repeatedly surrendered significant portions from the capital budget which is primarily meant for modernising the armed forces.

The intra service resource allocation reveals that while the Army spends highest percentage of its revenue expenditure on Pay and Allowances, the Navy and the Air Force spends mostly on stores. Unlike the Army, the Navy and to some extent the Air Force has been able to reduce their respective shares of Pay and Allowances in their revenue budgets.

In stores budget, while the Navy and the Air Force have nearly maintained their respective shares, there is a gradual decline in the case of the Army. Considering that the stores budget cater to among others, the operational readiness of the Armed Forces, the declining share of the Army's stores budget needs further probing for its adverse impact.

It is indeed a depressing observation that even after 64 years of independence India being the world's second fastest growing economy, one of the highest consumers of defence equipment, and a nation having the biggest reserve of technical manpower and scientific talent etc., is still dependent on foreign sources to meet 70% of its defence requirements.[10]

Even if a fraction of the large import bill is diverted towards indigenous production, the defence sector will be capable of generating large scale employment opportunities. As strategic analyst Brahma Chellaney rightly observes, India "invests bulk of its defence modernisation resources not on strengthening its own armament base or deterrent capabilities but on subsidizing the military industry complex of others."[11]

Relying on large scale imports to equip the defence forces militates against our larger national interests as many of the imported items are not suitable for operation under Indian climate and environmental conditions, their costs are prohibitive, continuity of supply and replenishment of spares is susceptible to political vagaries and the deals often trigger corruption and briberies in this vital area of national security.

Besides, they often entail high costs and time overruns and the possibilities of sanctions, technology denial and vexatious conditionality's make them unreliable.

Budget Planning and Defence Planning

The budgeting process should be closely linked with the defence planning process. Budgeting should be treated as the execution portion of defence planning cycle, so that there is close coordination between capability planning and budgeting. This will call for extended time horizon for defence budgeting as also change in the format of defence budget. Attention should be focused on the end products of defence budgeting through the concept of programmes for capability building, making it an output-oriented budget.

10. Ajit Doval, (Feb2012), "India's Defence Production and Research – Need for Transformational up-gradation", http://www.vifindia.org/article/2012/february/06/India-s-Defence-Production-and-Research-Need-for-Transformational-up-gradation. (Accessed in Feb2012)
11. Ibid.P. 2

Cost of Manpower

Apprehensions about the rising cost of Armed Forces manpower has been a topic of debate ever since the 5th and 6th Pay Commission recommendations were implemented in the 1994 and 2006. In the Defence Budget, manpower-associated costs are shown as Revenue Expenditure. The costs of modernising existing platforms, weapons and systems and acquiring of new ones are shown as Capital Expenditure.

It is important for the readers to understand that despite no significant growth in numbers, defence manpower the costs still continued to rise. The bill for today's ten lakh defence pensioners is 13,300 crores. It is due to the increasing trend of Voluntary Retirement Scheme (VRS) among the officers as they are being offered lucrative profile in the private sectors. This amount is more than six times the total annual manpower cost and constitutes 50 % of the Government of India's total pension bill. Defence pensioners increase by about one lakh every year – 60,000 to 70,000 Personnel below Officer Rank, 25,000 civilians and 1000 to 1200 officers.[12]

As the defence budget is unlikely to increase beyond 2.5 per cent of the GDP, the Army's modernisation plans have fallen way behind the required qualitative levels. It is said that there is a need to hunt for ground-breaking and resourceful solutions to reduce the costs of manpower even if the manpower itself cannot be reduced in large numbers at present.

As military manpower becomes more and more costly to recruit, train and retain, planners are increasingly opting for technological solutions at least in low risk areas and relying more on 'mean and lean' conventional forces for deterrence.

The reduction in conservative force level is leading to greater dependence on alliance warfare as nations contribute best of

---

12. Hiranandani G.M, (2011), 'Reconciling Manpower Costs', Indian Defence Review, http://www.indiandefencereview.com/news/reconciling-manpower-costs/ (Accessed in August 2013)

their capabilities to make for deficiencies and shortfalls and to gain diplomatic strength.

HIS Jane's consultancy, reckons that by 2020 India will overtake Japan, France and Britain at the global level.[13] However, it should be noticed that the reliance for manpower support in Britain and France is much simpler due to the pacts like North Atlantic Treaty Organisation (NATO). Therefore, this is not always the best solution, as alliances tend to have disparate motives and often lack cohesiveness.

And yet the most central defence planning challenges in all country remains the issue of how to harmonise the divergence which require a young fighting force, high standard of manpower and adequate career employment and advancement opportunities related to the socioeconomic and cultural factors specific to the country concerned.

Special efforts are being made to reduce the logistics footprint of armed forces by outsourcing the supply and maintenance chain to civilian trade wherever it can be done without compromising operational readiness.

It is now well recognised that a million strong army is unlikely to be unaffordable around the 2020-25 time frame unless modernisation is given the go by, because the costs of manpower are going up and the defence budget is continuing to decrease in constant Rupees year after year even as the cost of defence equipment is rising.

Therefore, it must now be accepted that qualitative upgradation of the whole army is possible only if quantitative re-sizing precedes it. At one level, the inability of the Indian Army to shed manpower is due to the lack of resources to replace it with high-end technologies, primarily because of the generally low

---

13. The Economist, (March 2013),"India as a great power Know your own strength" http://www.economist.com/news/briefing/21574458-india-poised-become-one-four-largest-military-powers-world-end. (Accessed in April 2013)

priority accorded to defence planning and inadequate resource allotment.

However the dichotomy here is the army cannot reduce manpower because of its commitments in low intensity conflict and it cannot modernise and improve the quality of the army cannot reduce manpower because of its commitments in low intensity conflict and it cannot modernise and improve the quality of its forces unless it reduces its manpower strength because its huge numbers are a drain on the defence its forces unless it reduces its manpower strength because its huge numbers are a drain on the defence budget.

Issue of Defence vs. Development

Nobel laureate Amartya Sen slams India's defence budget for harming the country's human development programmes. According to him the military expenditure is very high and affects key areas like health care and education, which requires massive investment. However it is blamed that due to the military build up the large chunk of the capital is diverted towards defence and the national social issues are neglected. Critics of excessive defence expenditure tend to view resources allocated towards security as a wasteful expenditure or at best a necessary evil. Thus the debate on defence vs. Development is never ending.[14]

In the light of the defence expenditure trend analysis, it is important to examine as to what proportion of GDP needs to be allocated to defence in the Indian context. As brought out during initial part of this chapter, the defence allocations as a percentage of the GDP have been declining over a period of time. It marked the figure of 3 percent in 1980s. However thereafter, this ratio came down to around 2.5 to 1.98 percent of GDP in recent years.[15]

14. Paranjpe Shrikant, (1993) 'Beyond the Defence and Development: A Framework for Analysis of Indian Expenditure', Mondes En Developpement-TOME21
15. Athawale Sanhita, (2004), 'Defence Services', New Delhi, Anmol Publications Pvt. Ltd.

I would like to draw the attention of the readers that India is not on any kind of extensive modernisation plan due to the shortcomings in its own procedures and guidelines. Also it is worth reading that India's defence budget has never crossed the limit of 2.5 percent of the GDP from the GDP growth of the nation at 4.7 percent.

According to Dr. Shrikant Paranjpe in his paper titled "Beyond the Defence and Development Debate: A framework for analysis of Indian defence expenditure" has said; 'A distinction must be made between the concept of development and the concept of economic growth. The former had a broader meaning that includes the political, economic and socio-cultural dimensions of human life. Consequently, a higher GNP may not be an indicator of development in a country. There is also the question of the correlation of the economic growth and defence expenditures.'[16]

In fact BENOIT's study concluded that higher military expenditures were more likely the cause rather that the effect of faster economic growth. He further argued that defence expenditure provided for skill enhancement, amelioration of infrastructure and helped to promote higher utilisation of existing productive capacity. It also ensures increased investments and employment opportunities.

The maximum portion of the defence budget is utilised by the pay and allowances department due to the central pay commissions that is applicable across the board for all the central government employees. Also this is an uncontrolled process as the Central Pay Commission comes after every 10 years gap.

The military is a symbol of power. And in order to hold this power and its manifestations, it is imperative that the allocations and upgradation of defence are enhanced in the years ahead.

---

16. Paranjpe Shrikant, (1993) 'Beyond the Defence and Development: A Framework for Analysis of Indian Expenditure', Mondes En Developpement-TOME21

Solutions to the Problems

In my view every organisation, think tank and the branded strategic analysis everyone has already talked enough about our challenges and problem in the system and where all it lack. Also they have alerted us many a times that we need to do something about us and only few odd thinkers have given us the viable solutions which are the need of the hour. In this section I will try and make an attempt to discuss certain solutions that if taken seriously can resolve some of our major issues.

First and most important is the ability to accept the truth. Indian government and Ministry of Defence must not close their eyes and avoid to face the music. It is a world known fact that Indian defences are at all time low and it will be better if the officials accept it. Instead of telling others who talk about it to be quite. **Because the more brave you will be to accept it, the more you will be in a position to rectify and answerable to others.** Just like we try to improve our personal standards and do the upgradation and renovation of our houses, similarly we need to be concerned about our defence system as well.

The obsolete equipment, delays in procurement, complicated procurement procedures and independence in training and poor or sub standards results in frustration, poor training, breeds incompetence's amongst the troops and not battle worthy or battle ready. There exists huge inferiority complex in the minds of soldiers, loss of self belief and confidence makes the issues larger than life in size.

Therefore in order to eliminate all such issues there is a need to enhance our capabilities through better defence budget and procurement which will directly improve the soldier's capability and regain the lost moral.

Thus most importantly the defence budget should be converted from allocated budget to demanded budget which should be based on the needs of the Armed Forces. **In the absence of the need based and programme oriented plan even the**

constraint of limited resources could not be applied rationally by determining relative inter-service and intra – service priorities.

In the past we have seen the idea of Five Year Defence Plan (FYDP) have not been feasible and fruitful; it is evident from the military preparedness and the slow moving modernisation plan. It is saddening to see that none of the five year plans could be completed for one or the other reason and had either been deferred or reframed midway.

However, the basic requirement in Indian defence budgeting and planning, as per budgeting parlance, is the requirements of programming budgeting, that is, the budget should be based on approved programmes. Instead of planning the defence programmes according o the budget allocated, the budget should be planned according to the defence plans.

We can put it in a Five Year framework as it is done in US and UK, but should be based on the rolling on concept. When the Five Year Defence Plan is based on the rolling basis, the question of financial commitment does not arise. In fact a rigid FYDP would force the policy makers in making the required changes in the programme on the basis of emerging developments in technology and rapidly changing security environment. The roll on planning will helps to serve as an action plan for achieving the strategic objectives.[17]

This rolling on of the FYDP is extension of the programme budgeting. It details what the department plans to request during the five year period and how it proposes to allocate its resources among the various investment and operating accounts.

An FYDP, particularly if it is prepared on a rolling basis, would be a necessary tool for the Defence Minister to give shape to the national security policy. A multi-layer plan that deals with forces

17. Ghosh Kumar Amiya (2006), 'Defence Five Year Plans and Defence Budget', Defence Budgeting and Planning in India: The Way Forward", New Delhi, Knowledge World

and costs in a comprehensive manner is necessary if the secretary of defence aims to achieve its national goals, indeed it is essential if there is to be a comprehensive and consistent policy.

Apart from the FYDP based on the roll on practice, the option of programme budgeting is also viable solution to confront the main lacuna in the budgeting system.

As Greenwood stated, "where expenditure plans have been planned for a sequence of future years- i.e. a time profile of intended outlays has been drawn up the expenditure related to functions or outputs, then there exists a programme budget."[18]

Multi-year expenditure plans and multi-year budgeting on a roll-on basis are the main aspect of programming budgeting. It gives emphasis to the "planning" function of budgeting and updating the plan with addition of another year in it.

Kaufman states' "but despite its provisional nature, the programme is meant to force policy makers to think seriously and systematically about the future. If conscientiously implemented, the FYDP minimises the probability that 'foot-in-the-door' tactics can be used to shoehorn new and potentially budget-busting weapons into the budget".[19]

Programme planning and programme budgeting involves detailed costing of the existing programme and the proposed programme. It indicates foreseeable implications of current decisions. It enables decision makers to see the costs of the proposed new programme over a period of years. It is necessary as it would help in economic analysis of military problems and controls the last minute changes in the plans.

It should be of the Defence, for the defence and by the defence. It should be presented separately and before the rest of the budget for the Fiscal year in the parliament. While the Defence

18. Ghosh Kumar Amiya (2006), 'Defence Five Year Plans and Defence Budget', Defence Budgeting and Planning in India: The Way Forward", New Delhi, Knowledge World
19. Ibid. p. 234

Minister of India is presenting the budget the Chiefs from the three services and the defence secretary should be presented in the Lok Sabah. This is practical and possible step that the military and politicians should attempt to imply together.

The commanders in the Army, Navy and Air Force should be given more decision making powers. As they are the ones who are fighting with the existing issues and can asses better in matters of how to overcome the problem and control the situation. Also our chiefs being the leader of the services should have the courage to stand and speak in favour of their men and organisation rather than their personal interests. If in today's time our chiefs stand against the acquisition of outdated and corrupt equipments from other countries (their trash), then we will not face loss of so many Indian soldiers and officers. Hence it must be pointed and the idea must be spread that we should start valuing the human lives.

Instead of simply praising the United States of America for their determination and respect for human life we must understand that how closely they associate themselves with each and every man in their Army.

Therefore, our policies and doctrines should be offensive in nature rather than a defensive and passive reactive planning in nature.

Our country should formulate a strategic defence review every year which is formed by the serving officers and civil servants comprising of the elaborative report on the aims, resources results and suggestions which should be implemented by the politicians. It implies that the civil-military relations should be reshaped based on present scenario keeping aside self interest of the senior officials in both the civil and military community. Balancing this act will reduce half of the irritants from the organisation.

To match the standards of defence weapons and equipment at the global level, India needs to adopted a policy of upgradation of the defence weapons and equipments on the priority bases with the 40:30:30 ratios in which the 40 should be the procurement of the latest equipment, 30 should be the scrapping of the obsolete weapon which has completed its operational life cycle and finally the last 30 should be the planning and management of the near future obsolescing weapons and equipments. It will ensure better utility of the defence expenditure provided.

The phase wise modernisation plan should be started for each service (Army, Navy and Air Force) to avoid any kind of overlapping in the executions and to reduce waiting time for all delivery of new equipments and weapons. These phase wise/ service wise modernisation plan should further be based on fixed time period for 5 years. This will ensure timely execution to avoid any kind of penalty from the auditors and monitoring agencies. It will also ensure that the pressure deliberately and persistently exists in the office to produce quality work in fixed timeline.

Further the gestation period from the time of the conceptualisation of the equipment to the final execution and utilisation of the product, should be as little as possible in order to avoid the surrender the fund back to the Ministry of Finance and ensure execution of the procurement plan in time bound phase. Also in order to ensure this ruling stringent actions should be taken against the authorities involved in the process for any kind of delays and malfunctioning.

In order to control the surrender of the unspent defence budget we need to fix accountability of the MoD there is need to have an integrated acquisition system with all the related functions carried under the supervision of the senior commander who should be changed with every new procurement project in order to avoid any kind of malpractices. There is also a need to have a dedicated pool of personnel who are well versed in acquisition task which should comprise of the uniformed officers in order to have the facts from the ground zero.

The government should formulate a Special Expedition Sanctioning Process (SESP) which should lay in the hands of the chiefs of Army, Navy and Air Force or anyone who is the highest in command. This implies that just in case the politicians or the ministry of Finance is unable to pass the proposal due to over work or pressure of too many issues then in that case the senior commander should have the right to pass the project and expedite the procurement or production.

Next aim should be to establish a Special Military Economic Zone (SMEZ) on the lines of Special Economic Zones (SEZ) at minimum four places in the Eastern, Western, Northern and Southern zones. In ach zone the products should be developed, invented, produced for the forces stationed there and should be tested there itself and if successful should be produced at large scale. This will save the time and money in production, transportation from place A to B.

Further these SMEZ can employ or work in close contact with the major IT companies of India or can be a contractual hiring for a time period. With the fast improving satellite based infra red and photographic sensors for strategic intelligence and availability of sensor-laden drones for tactical intelligence in the battlefield, India needs to increase its pace of working. One way to swiftly bridge the gap may be to involve the country's private sector IT more actively to develop the software and attendant technologies.

India is far away from any such capability but with sufficient investment in a series of low altitude micro-satellites- perhaps in a joint development and launch programme with Israel- to match the Indian satellite building capability for medium altitude and geo-synchronous earth orbiters; this may not be unachievable in the next three decades.

These SMEZ can also be offered to the other countries for testing their products and conducting research. This will not only help us in getting to know the others countries progress in the field of technology but also improve our business relations with them. These relations can prove helpful in peace time and at the time of crisis as well.

Also the merging of the logistics and intelligence webs of the three services into separate commands under the ministry of defence to avoid the duplication and multiplication of such support establishments

Several possible options can be taken into consideration to reduce the strength of the standing army without overlooking the operational preparedness though each one of these suggestions would need to be thought through sensibly to get rid of any kind of disadvantages involved. Large-scale Territorial Army can offer a lucrative opportunity to save on manpower costs by reducing the number of regular army personnel in service and increasing the number of Territorial Army (TA) personnel.

The idea is to convert some regular Indian Army units to Territorial Army units. Besides infantry battalions, Corps of Army Air Defence TA units have existed in the past in India. Even today the British Army, that has been downsized and has only two deployable active service divisions, places immense reliance on TA units for almost all arms and services.

In the initial stages the concept could be tried out with some units which are not immediately involved in military operations like the Army Air Defence. It may be more prudent to convert one or two rifle companies to TA companies rather than convert a whole battalion. When the concept is found to be successful, it could be extended to other arms like the armoured corps, artillery, Corps of Army Air Defence, signals, Engineers and the mechanised infantry.

Since all of these arms have equipment-intensive holdings, innovative methods will have to be devised to keep the TA soldiers trained in handling their equipment and to ensure that the equipment is well maintained.

The TA personnel's will be trained based on the individual's educational qualification and capabilities which will be assessed by the tests before hand. For example if the personnel who is educationally qualified as a civil engineer or the mechanical engineer, then he/she will be trained to be inducted in the Corp of Engineer or in the unit of Electric Mechanical Engineer (EME) respectively. Similarly in case of the communication engineer the personnel will be given training about the Corp of Signal. This can also be done in the Navy and Air Force at least for the ground duties.

In this way not only our forces will multiply in number but the cost of up keeping the permanent force will be reduced to a large extent. For the same there should be a tie up between the private sector and the armed forces to give the permission to the TA officers to release for the services in the eleventh hour during crisis without any legal or procedural barrier. And also these TA officers training should be refreshed at regular intervals.

This would require bold political initiative, from which none of the national political party concerned with the nation's interest should flinch. Unless some of these measures are adopted, manpower costs will continue to bite into the meagre funds available for military modernisation.

To ensure savings in manpower costs enactment of a new legal Act is required with stringent provisions for ensuring that the large mass of the youth of this nation serve in the armed forces on a mandatory basis. This is similar to the concept which is there in NATO countries. The youth from colleges and universities should be inducted and trained for minimum 2 years.

This will not only build our reserve manpower but also bring about the change in the mindset and discipline in the country. This method was very normal during the World War and other international wars and has proved to less monetary oriented. These students from the colleges and universities should be provided with similar facilities as a regular soldier is provided to him and his family till the time he/she is in the armed forces i.e. 2 years. In a way it can prove to be a future solution to the existing shortage of the officers in the army.

Another solution which has been practically tested in other countries is the visible build up in the force levels of Special Forces the world over. As greater reliance is being placed on the low-visibility employment of military force. Like China's Blue Force which is formed and trained to fight against a particular kind of forces and under certain environment, similarly, the US Navy Seals which are world famous for the conduct of an 'Operation Geronimo'.

On the same line India should also plan and coordinate to raise a special forces which already exists in the nation but needs to develop and improve to a large extent. They should be trained in anti-guerrilla and anti-terrorist actions, fight minor bushfire wars and be the lead element in effecting rapid intervention-these being the sorts of conflict scenario most likely to obtain here on. They need to feature more than a para troop type of unit.

The another significant point to be implemented is that the Integrated Financial Advisor (IFA) should be a uniformed personnel or else in case of the civil servant the official should be send to the forwards areas for the period of 2 years on the peace-field pattern. So that the civil officer acquaints itself with the ground realities of the situation existing and accordingly advise and plan the budgeting for the armed forces.

No doubt there will be significant struggle within the army on the execution of such a concept. Heads of the Corps and units with deeply fixed mindsets will warn against the dangers of such a venture and will question the operational preparedness of such units even after a three to six month warning period for training.

However, if we take these steps on the lines of lab experiment without any kind of hitch it can prove to be helpful. Time has come and it will be better for the army to begin planning its implementation in house rather than have it imposed from without. It will not be easy concept to implement and many challenges will have to be overcome, but then nothing new is ever easy. In case of any new thing being introduced there is always some yes and some no.

Another major evolution in the strategic planning can be introduced by establishing something like Defence Advanced Research Projects Agency (DARPA) which was earlier called as the Advanced Research Projects Agency (ARPA) created in 1958 by the United States Department of Defence responsible for the development of new technologies for us by the military. It is responsible for funding the development of many technologies which have had major effect on the world, including computer networking and Online System (NLS).

It was created in response to the Soviet launching of Sputnik 1 in 1957, and then ARPA and now DARPA's mission was to ensure U.S military technology be more sophisticated than that of the nation's potential enemies. [20]

From DARPA's own introduction:

DARPA's original mission, established in 1958, was to prevent technological surprise like the launch of Sputnik, which signalled that the Soviets had beaten the U.S. into space. The mission statement has evolved over time. Today, DARPA's mission is still to prevent technological surprise to the US, but also to create technological surprise for our enemies.

DARPA is independent from other more conventional military research and development and reports directly to senior Department of Defence management. DARPA has around 240 personnel (about 140 technical) directly managing a $2.8 billion budget. These figures are "on average" since DARPA focuses on short-term (two to four year) projects run by small, purpose-built teams.

---

20. Defence Advanced Research Project Agency (DARPA), Home page, http://www.darpa.mil/default.aspx (Accessed in February 2014)

Something like this comes in India, then the capability and standards of research and development will take a giant leap towards betterment. If we look at the characteristics of DARPA, all kinds of doubts related to system management will be clarified. Therefore, it is worth having a attentive read on some key features of DARPA:

- *Small and flexible:* DARPA has only about 140 technical professionals; DARPA presents itself as "100 geniuses connected by a travel agent.
- *Flat organization:* DARPA avoids hierarchy, essentially operating at only two management levels to ensure the free and rapid flow of information and ideas, and rapid decision-making.
- *Autonomy and freedom from bureaucratic impediments:* DARPA has an exemption from Title V civilian personnel specifications, which provides for a direct authority to hire talents with the expediency not allowed by the standard civil service processes.
- *Eclectic, world-class technical staff and performers:* DARPA seeks great talents and ideas from industry, universities, government laboratories, and individuals, mixing disciplines and theoretical and experimental strength. DARPA neither owns nor operates any laboratories or facilities, and the overwhelming majority of the research it sponsors is done in industry and universities. Very little of DARPA's research is performed at government labs.
- *Teams and networks:* At its very best, DARPA creates and sustains great teams of researchers from different disciplines that collaborate and share in the teams' advances.
- *Hiring continuity and change:* DARPA's technical staff is hired or assigned for four to six years. All key staff i.e. Office Directors and Program Managers are rotated to ensure constant infusion of fresh thinking and perspectives.
- *Project-based assignments organized around a challenge model:* DARPA organizes a significant part of its portfolio around

specific technology challenges. It foresees innovation-based capabilities and then works back to the fundamental breakthroughs required to make them possible. Although individual projects typically last three to five years, major technological challenges may be addressed over longer time periods, ensuring patient investment on a series of focused steps and keeping teams together for ongoing collaboration.

- *Outsourced support personnel:* DARPA extensively leverages technical, contracting, and administrative services from other DoD agencies and branches of the military. This provides DARPA the flexibility to get into and out of an area without the burden of sustaining staff, while building cooperative alliances with its "agents." These outside agents help create a constituency in their respective organizations for adopting the technology.
- *Outstanding program managers:* The best DARPA program managers have always been freewheeling zealots in pursuit of their goals. The Director's most important task is to recruit and hire very creative people with big ideas, and empower them.
- *Acceptance of failure:* DARPA pursues breakthrough opportunities and is very tolerant of technical failure if the payoff from success will be great enough.
- *Orientation to revolutionary breakthroughs in a connected approach:* DARPA historically has focused not on incremental but radical innovation. It emphasizes high-risk investment, moves from fundamental technological advances to prototyping, and then hands off the system development and production to the military services or the commercial sector.
- *Mix of connected collaborators:* DARPA typically builds strong teams and networks of collaborators, bringing in a range of technical expertise and applicable disciplines, and involving university researchers and technology firms that

are often not significant defence contractors or beltway consultants. [21]

The issue with the ***military farm*** is another issue which needs the attention of the decision makers and policy planners. The Army HQ should close down its 39 military farms, which house around 23,600 cattle with an annual production of over 335 lakh kg of milk, in two phases. Cantonments were earlier largely isolated from towns and cities. But with rapid urban growth, most cantonment are now located within population clusters. Moreover, after the green and white revolutions, there is no dearth of milk and milk products from civilian sources now. Military farms have lost their relevance. The operation of military farms, which rear livestock, vegetables, fodder and fertilizers under an annual Rs 374 crore budget, has also been flawed by major corruption cases and some officers being court-martialled in recent years.[22]

When the military farms will be shut down then, almost 2,000 personnel of the military farms, including over 20 officers, will also be progressively transferred to other wings and departments or managed outside the organisation will help in reducing the cost on manpower as well.

We must remember that there is no simple solution to the complex set of problems that arise in relation to the national defence. However what can be attempted is to search for the direction to proceed especially if we are to ensure that a war is not imposed again on us through misperceptions and under preparedness.

The plans outlined above may sound platonic or loud thinking, but it basically aims to develop a strategic oriented planning.

---

21. Defence Advanced Research Project Agency (DARPA), Home page, http://www.darpa.mil/default.aspx (Accessed in February 2014)
22. PanditRajat, (2013), 'All Military Farms to be Shut Shops by 2017', Times of India, http://timesofindia.indiatimes.com/india/All-military-farms-to-shut-shop-by-2017/articleshow/19668690.cms (Accessed in August 2013)

There are no soft alternatives to converting the Indian military into strategic force of consequence capable of forcefully backing the country's larger political objectives. This conversion of the military standards no doubt involves the high cost of enforcement but it is nothing that cannot be paid by the exchequers of this country.

It should be kept in mind that the theory of time itself is the most significant/prime dimension of the war in today's time. Hence we should grow above the past and instead of time and again referring to the wars fought by India against China and Pakistan in 1962, 1965, 1971 and so on. Instead we need to look forward plan form the lessons learnt from the failures and improve for the future.

The parliament attack, 26/11 attack in Mumbai meant lot of opportunities for the armed forces to advance its inventory, equipments and weapons but due to lack of foresightedness and motivation, it caused backlog and left us way behind the rest of the world. Even though Armed Forces have been trying to indulge in new practices which give us satisfactory results but then it goes down the drain. The reason is that no one is creating new ideas; it is simply colour coating of the same practice and giving it a new name. The functioning still remains the same.

The onus is upon us to understand that it if don't wake up from the slumber we will again be in shackles of the world. More than, simply increasing the voice for budget, along with that we need to first ignite our mind and think about life of men in uniform.

Hence, it is very vital to understand that "it is very essential to think out of box about the box, because we cannot remain in the box to think about the box".

Appendix

The weapons and Equipments of India Defence Services

This section contains the list of the modern and historical equipments of the Indian Armed Forces. Most of the army equipment is of foreign design and license produced in India but efforts are on to progressively design and manufacture equipment indigenously.

Chart 1: Ballistic and Cruise

Name	Type	Origin	Notes
Brahmos	Stealth Cruise missile	India Russia	300 km range.
Prahaar	Tactical ballistic missile	India	150 km range.
Prithvi-I	Short-range ballistic missile	India	150 km range. (Being Phased Out)
Prithvi-II	Short-range ballistic missile	India	250 – 350 km range.
Prithvi-III	Short-range ballistic missile	India	350 – 600 km range.
Shaurya	Medium-range ballistic missile	India	700 km range.
Agni-I	Medium-range ballistic missile	India	700 – 1250 km range.

Name	Type	Origin	Notes
Agni-II	Intermediate-range ballistic missile	India	2000 – 3500 km range.
Agni-III	Intermediate-range ballistic missile	India	3500 – 5000 km range.
Agni-IV	Intermediate-range ballistic missile	India	4000 – 6000 km range.
Agni-V	Intercontinental ballistic missile	India	5000 – 8000 km range

(**Source:** Wikipedia)

Chart 2: UAVs

Aircraft	Origin	Type	Versions	Quantity
IAI Heron	Israel	Unmanned aerial vehicle		50+
DRDO Nishant	India	Unmanned aerial vehicle		12+
IAI Searcher	Israel	Unmanned aerial vehicle	Searcher II Searcher I	120+

(**Source:** Wikipedia)

Chart 3: Air defence

Name	Type	Origin	Notes
Prithvi Air Defense (PAD)	Anti-ballistic missile	India	Exoatmospheric (outside the atmosphere) interceptor system
Advanced Air Defence (AAD)	Anti-ballistic missile	India	Endo atmospheric (within the atmosphere) interceptor system
S-300PMU-2	Strategic Surface-to-air missile	Russia	Still officially unacknowledged.
SA-5 Gammon	Strategic SAM system	Soviet Union	Still officially unacknowledged.

Name	Type	Origin	Notes
SA-3 Goa	Strategic SAM system	Soviet Union	It is designed to defend large areas from bomber attack or other strategic aircraft.
Akash	Surface-to-air missile	India	More on Order. Indigenously developed surface to air missile to replace SA6. Both with Army and Air Force
Kub (SA-6 Gainful)	Surface-to-air missile	Soviet Union	
9K33 Osa (SA-8 Gecko)	6x6 amphibious Surface-to-air missile system	Russia	
9K31 Strela-1 (SA-9 Gaskin)	Vehicle-mounted SAM system	Soviet Union	
9K35 Strela-10 (SA-13 Gopher)	Surface-to-air missile	Soviet Union	
S-75 Dvina (SA-2 Guideline)	Strategic SAM system	Soviet Union	
9K22 Tunguska[58]	Self-propelled anti-aircraft weapon	Russia	
ZSU-23-4M 'Shilka'	Self-propelled anti-aircraft gun	Soviet Union	To be upgraded.
Bofors L40/70	Anti-aircraft artillery	Sweden	40mm gun. Upgraded L/60. To be replaced by 430 domestically-built anti-aircraft gun systems.
Bofors L40/60	Anti-aircraft artillery	Sweden	40mm gun. To be replaced.
ZSU-23-2	Anti-aircraft artillery	Soviet Union	Twin 23 mm AA gun
SA-16 Gimlet	MANPADS	Soviet Union	

Name	Type	Origin	Notes
SA-7 Grail	MANPADS	Russia	To be phased out.
FIM-92 Stinger	MANPADS	United States	245
SA-14 Gremlin	MANPADS	Russia	
SA-18 Grouse	MANPADS	Russia	

Chart 4: Mine Protected, Mine Clearing and Mine Laying

Name	Type	Origin	Notes
Casspir	Armoured personnel carrier	South Africa	
Tarmour AFV	Armoured personnel carrier	India	Based on Indian T-55 Tank.
Hydrema	Mine clearing Vehicle	Denmark India	Manufactured locally by OFB India
T-72 FWMP	Mine plow	India	
Aditya	Mine protected Vehicle	India	OFB India. 1400 to be produced. 20/month manufactured at Ordnance Factory MedakAND Vehicle Factory Jabalpur.
DRDO Daksh	Bomb disposal robot	India	The Army has placed orders for 200 Dakshs.

(**Source:** Wikipedia)

Chart 5: Explosives, Rockets and Missile Systems

Name	Type	Origin	Notes
Grenade 36mm	Hand Grenade	India	Fragmentation grenade which can be hand thrown or rifle launched from 1A SLR.
Multi Mode Grenade Shivalik	Hand grenade	India	This modular grenade is available in Hand mode offensive, hand mode defensive and rifle mode. Types can be interchanged by changing outer sleeve.
Multi Grenade Launcher 40mm	Grenade launcher (40mm)	India	Semiautomatic six shot 40mm x 46mm low velocity grenade launcher. Manufactured at Ordnance Factory Tiruchirappalli.

Name	Type	Origin	Notes
GP-25	Grenade launcher (40mm)	Soviet Union	
36M	Grenade launcher (61mm)	India United Kingdom	
RPO-A Shmel	Rocket Launcher	Russia	
36M Mk.I	Rifle grenade	United Kingdom	
AGS-17 Plamya	Automatic grenade launcher (30mm)	Soviet Union	
30 mm Auto Grenade Launcher	Automatic grenade launcher (30mm)	India	Replacing the AGS-17 and being manufactured at Ordnance Factory Tiruchirappalli.
RCL Mk II	Recoilless rifle (84mm)	India Sweden	Carl Gustav Recoilless Rifle produced by OFB.
RCL Mk III	Recoilless rifle (84mm)	India Sweden	Lighter, updated version of the RCL Mk II.
106 mm M-40A1	Recoilless rifle	United States	
RPG-7	Rocket propelled grenade (40mm)	Soviet Union	
RPG-22	Rocket propelled grenade (72.5mm)	Soviet Union	
OFB E1 51mm	Mortar	India	
OFB E1 81mm	Mortar	India	
L16 81mm mortar		United Kingdom Canada	
OFB E1 81mm	HE Bomb Smoke Bomb	India	

Name	Type	Origin	Notes
OFB E1 120mm	Mortar HE Bomb	India	
120mm AM-50	Mortar HE Bomb	France	
160 mm Tampella	Mortar	Finland	
Shipon	Rocket launcher (82mm)	Israel	

(**Source:** Wikipedia)

Chart 6: Indian Air Force

Aircraft	Origin	Role	Comment
Sukhoi Su-30MKI	Russia India	Air superiority fighter	Total 272 on order (to be delivered by 2018). All aircraft to be upgraded to "Super Sukhoi" status. Upgrades would include AESA radar among other things.
Mikoyan MiG-29	Soviet Union	Air superiority fighter	To be Upgraded to MiG-29UPG Standard.
HAL Tejas	India	Multirole fighter	8 delivered with 40 more on order. Total 294 Mk I and Mk II aircraft may be ordered to equip 14 squadrons to replace the MiG-21 and MiG-27 fleets.
Dassault Mirage 2000	France	Multirole fighter	59 Mirage 2000's including 10 trainers were acquired. The current fleet of 49 will be upgraded to Mirage 2000-5 Mk2 standard between 2011 and 2020.
Mikoyan-Gurevich MiG-21	Soviet Union India	Fighter aircraft	125 Upgraded Bisons to be phased out by 2025. Mig-21 FL was phased out in December 2013.
Mikoyan-Gurevich MiG-27 Bahadur	Soviet Union	Ground - attack aircraft	To be phased out by 2017.

Aircraft	Origin	Role	Comment
SEPECAT Jaguar	France United Kingdom	Ground - attack aircraft	Undergoing upgrades to prolong service life.
C-17 Globemaster	United States	Strategic transport	5 more on order.
Ilyushin Il-76 Candid	Soviet Union	Strategic transport	
C-130J Super Hercules	United States	Tactical transport	6 more ordered in December 2013.
Hawker Siddeley HS 748	United Kingdom India	Tactical transport	To be replaced under a $2.4 billion program.
Antonov An-32 Cline	Soviet Union	Light tactical transport	A light, short ranged tactical transport. Currently being upgraded in Ukraine to prolong service life.
Boeing 737	United States	Airliner (passenger)	One 737-200 ADV and Three 737-700 BBJ1 used for VIP transport.
Dornier Do 228	Germany India	Utility transport	
IAI Astra 1125	Israel	VIP transport	
Beriev A-50 Phalcon	Israel Russia	Airborne early warning & control	2 more on order.
EMB-145 AEWCS	Brazil India	Airborne early warning & control	3 ordered, with one delivered. Undergoing testing by DRDO and IAF. All 3 expected to be in service by 2015.
Ilyushin Il-78 MKI	Russia	Aerial refuelling	
Gulfstream III	United States	Reconnaissance	
BAE Hawk	United Kingdom India	Trainer aircraft	53 more on order.

Aircraft	Origin	Role	Comment
HAL HJT-16 Kiran	India	Trainer aircraft	To be phased out by 2017.
Pilatus PC-7	Switzer-land	Trainer aircraft	75 ordered, with a possible order for another 37, and a follow up order of an additional 100.
HAL HPT-32 Deepak	India	Trainer aircraft	Current fleet of around 70 aircraft grounded. Being replaced by Pilatus PC-7 trainer aircraft, of which 75 have been ordered.
HAL Rudra	India	Attack helicopter	Total of 16 on order.
HAL Light Combat Helicopter	India	Attack helicopter	65 on order.
Mil Mi-35 Hind-E	Soviet Union	Military helicopter	Will be replaced by 22 Boein-gAH-64 Apache attack helicopters.
Mil Mi-8 Mi-17	Soviet Union	Transport helicopter	19 Mi-17V5 delivered by February 2014, of the total 59 ordered for the Air Force in December 2012.
Mil Mi-26 Halo	Soviet Union	Transport helicopter	Will be complemented by Boe-ingCH-47 Chinook of which 15 is being ordered.
Agust-aWestland AW101	Italy	Transport helicopter	12 originally planned, however deal was cancelled in January 2014 due to corruption charges.
HAL Dhruv	India	Utility helicopter	65 more on order.
HAL Chee-tah	France India	Utility helicopter	
HAL Che-tak	France India		

Chart 7: Indian Naval Air Arms

Aircraft	Origin	Role	Comment
Mikoyan MiG-29K	Russia	Multirole fighter	All are delivered
BAE Sea Harrier	United Kingdom	Fighter aircraft	V/STOL

Aircraft	Origin	Role	Comment
Boeing P-8 Poseidon	United States	Maritime patrol aircraft	9 more on order.
Tupolev Tu-142	Soviet Union	Maritime patrol aircraft	Being replaced by 12 Boeing P-8 Poseidon.
Ilyushin Il-38 May	Soviet Union	Maritime patrol aircraft	
Dornier Do 228	Germany India	Utility aircraft	6 more on order.
BAE Hawk	United Kingdom	Trainer aircraft	13 more on order.
HAL HJT-16 Kiran	India	Trainer aircraft	
Kamov Ka-31 Helix-B	Russia	Airborne early warning	
Westland Sea King	United Kingdom	Anti-submarine warfare	
		Search & Rescue, utility transport	
Sikorsky SH-3 Sea King	United States	Anti-submarine warfare, utility transport	
Kamov Ka-25 Hormone	Soviet Union	Anti-submarine warfare	
Kamov Ka-28 Helix-A	Russia	Anti-submarine warfare	
HAL Chetak	France India	Utility helicopter	
HAL Dhruv	India	Utility helicopter	More on order.

(**Source:** Wikipedia)

Chart 8: Army Aviation Corps

Aircraft	Origin	Role	Version
HAL Rudra	India	Attack helicopter	ALH-WSI
HAL Light Combat Helicopter	India	Attack helicopter	LCH

Aircraft	Origin	Role	Version
HAL Lancer	France India	Light attack helicopter	
Mi-17V Hip	Soviet Union	Transport Helicopter	
HAL Dhruv	India	Utility helicopter	
HAL Chetak	France India	Utility helicopter	SA 316B Chetak
HAL Cheetah	France India	Utility helicopter	SA 315B Cheetah
			HAL Cheetal

Chart 9: Indian Coast Guard

Aircraft	Origin	Role
Dornier Do 228	India Germany	Maritime surveillance, search and rescue
HAL Dhruv	India	Utility helicopter
HAL Chetak	India France	Utility helicopter

Chart 10: Unmanned Aerial Vehicles (UAV)

The Indian Armed Forces operate a number of unmanned aerial vehicles split between the three service branches.

Aircraft	Origin	Role	Comment
IAI Harpy	Israel	Unmanned combat air vehicle	A small UCAV that homes into enemy radar emissions - destroying both itself and the enemy radar. In service with Indian Air Force.
IAI Harop	Israel	Unmanned combat air vehicle	A small UCAV that homes into enemy radar emissions - destroying both itself and the enemy radar. In service with Indian Air Force.
IAI Heron	Israel	Unmanned aerial vehicle	In service with Indian Air Force and Indian Navy. 15 more ordered in December 2013.

Aircraft	Origin	Role	Comment
DRDO Lakshya	India	Target drone	A small target drone in service with the Indian Air Force and Indian Navy.
DRDO Nishant	India	Unmanned aerial vehicle	In service with the Indian Army.
IAI Searcher	Israel	Unmanned aerial vehicle	In service with the Indian Army.

(**Source:** Wikipedia)

Future Procurements

Vehicles

- Kroton – Possible sale of 80 mine laying vehicles from Poland.
- Light Tank – 300 tanks (200 tracked 100 wheeled) to be deployed on China border.
- AHS Krab – Possible sale of 110 from Poland. Part of the deal that would also see the purchase of the Kroton and Loara.
- PZA Loara Possible sale of 100 from Poland. Part of the deal that would also see the purchase of the Kroton and 2S1 Gvozdika.
- BMP-2 based AKASH SAM carrier production started at Ordnance Factory Medak.
- BMP-2 based 105mm Light tank to be manufactured at Ordnance Factory Medak.
- BMP-2 based NBC protected recon vehicle to be manufactured at Ordnance Factory Medak.
- TATA Light Specialist Vehicle – LSV with LMG, MMG to be purchased

Artillery and missile systems

- Anti-tank missile FGM-148 Javelin and Spike (missile) are being evaluated currently by Indian Army.

- Under the Field Artillery Rationalization Plan, Indian Army plans to procure 3000 to 4000 155 mm towed, wheeled and tracked artillery systems. The requirement for artillery guns to be met with indigenous development and production. Production of crucial bi-modular charge system will be started soon at Nalanda ordnance factory. HEMRL, a DRDO lab has developed the technology indigenously.
- State-run Ordnance Factory Board (OFB) will deliver two types of indigenously developed 155mm howitzers to the Indian Army based on the FH77B howitzer purchased way back in 1986. One version will be 155/39 calibre while the other will be 155/45 calibre. Trials are to be completed by June 2013
- Government is also evaluating 155mm/52 self-propelled howitzers wherein three Indian vendors, including two private sector companies, have been selected for trials of their equipment. This information was given by Defence Minister Shri AK Antony in a written reply to Shri Ramesh Bais and others in Lok Sabha on 6-May-2013.
- Shaurya
- Prahaar- the solid-fuelled missile is slated to replace the liquid fuelled Prithvi-1. Liquid-fuelled missiles have lengthy preparation times giving adequate warning to the enemy, while solid-fueled ones can be ready in minutes.
- Agni-IV
- Agni-V – Intercontinental version of the Agni missile system. The missile was test fired for the first time on 19 April 2012 and is expected to be inducted by 2014–15.

Infantry equipment

- Futuristic Infantry Soldier As a System (F-INSAS) is the Indian Army's principal modernisation program from 2012 to 2020. In the first phase, to be completed by 2012,the infantry soldiers will be equipped with modular weapon systems that will have multi-functions. The Indian Army intends to modernise its entire 465 infantry and paramilitary battalions by 2020 with this program.

- A deal worth $5.75 million was signed with M/S B&T Switzerland for the acquisition of 1,568 advanced sub-machine guns for the Ghatak platoons of the army's infantry battalions.
- Modern Sub Machine Carbine - to replace the Indian Sterling submachine gun.
- Indian Army has requirement for 300,000 modular body armour and ballistic helmets primarily for their Infantry regiments. RFI's have been issued.
- 1000 Anti materiel rifles are to acquired for which global RFI's have been issued by the MOD.
- Army has issued RFI's for multi-caliber assault rifles probably to be used as the weapon system in the F-INSAS program.
- Indian army is looking for a heavy machine gun, RFIs for a new HMG have been sent to agencies that include Rosoboron export for the Degtyarev Kord 12.7mm HMG, General Dynamics for the still in-development M806 HMG and also the Browning M2E50.

Aviation

- **Light Utility Helicopter:** The Indian army has projected a requirement for up to 197 light helicopters to replace its ageing fleet of Chetaks and Cheetahs. The Indian Army chose the Eurocopter AS 550 under a US$550 million contract in summer of 2007. Under this contract 60 helicopters were to be supplied from Eurocopter in fly-away condition and the rest were to be assembled by HAL in India. This order was later scrapped due to allegations of unfair field trials from competing company Bell Helicopters.
- **Light Combat Helicopter:** The HAL Light Combat Helicopter is a derivative of the HAL Dhruv, which was

inducted into the Indian armed forces. Using a successful and proven helicopter as the base platform is expected to conserve the project costs for the LCH, which is pegged at 3.76 billion (US$61.3 million). The Dhruv's weaponised version, HAL Rudra is also being inducted in the Indian Army. The LCH was expected to be ready for the Initial Operational Clearance (IOC) by December 2010 with the Final Operational Clearance (FOC) in 2011. However, the revised timeframes hold that the 5.5-tonne LCH should be ready for induction into IAF by 2012–2013. The first prototype of LCH completed its first ground run on 4 February 2010. HAL has a firm order to deliver 65 LCH to the IAF and 114 to the Army.

- **Light multi-role helicopter:**
  Five global helicopter majors are in the fray to sell India 197 multi-role, light helicopters, in a deal worth 30 billion. Eurocopter AS550 Fennec; Kamov Ka-226, Agusta A109 Power or A119 Koala and McDonnell Douglas Helicopter Systems (MD 520N) have been given time till 19 December 2008 to submit proposals. Weighing less than three tonnes when armed, these multi-role, light turbine helicopters will replace the 1970s vintage Chetak and Cheetah helicopters operated by the Army Aviation Corps and the Air Force. They will undertake tasks such as reconnaissance and observation, casualty evacuation, electronic warfare, escort duties, anti-insurgency operations and ferrying personnel to and from the battlefield. Of the 197 helicopters, which are to be bought in a fly away condition and via knock down kits, 133 are for the Army, while 64 will be delivered to the Air Force. The helicopter deal is part of a mega modernisation programme which will see the Army eventually receiving 197 helicopters and the Indian Air Force getting 188. The deal also includes an offset clause, under which the successful vendor must source defence-related goods and services to the value of 50 per cent of the deal from Indian companies.

List of Active Indian Navy Ships

The Indian Navy is one of the largest navies in the world, and as of 2014 possesses two aircraft carriers, one amphibious transport dock, 9 Landing ship tanks, 8 destroyers, 15 frigates, one nuclear-powered attack submarine, 14 conventionally-powered attack submarines, 24 corvettes, 7 mine countermeasure vessels, 9 large offshore patrol vessels, 4 fleet tankers and various auxiliary vessels and small patrol boats.

Submarine Fleet

Chart 11: Nuclear-powered submarines

Class	Type	Boats	Origin	Note
Chakra (Akula II)-class	Attack submarine (SSN)	INS Chakra (S71)	Russia	Under a 10 year lease from Russia since 2012.
Arihant-class	Ballistic Missile submarine (SSBN)	INS Arihant (S73)	India	Undergoing sea trials, expected to be commissioned by 2014-2015.

Chart 12: Conventionally-Powered Submarines

Class	Type	Boats	Origin	Note
Sindhughosh-class	Attack submarine	INS Sindhughosh (S55) INS Sindhudhvaj (S56) INS Sindhuraj (S57) INS Sindhuvir (S58) INS Sindhuratna (S59) INS Sindhukesari (S60) INS Sindhukirti (S61) INS Sindhuvijay (S62) INS Sindhurakshak (S63) INS Sindhushastra (S65)	Soviet Union	S63 Sindhurakshak exploded and sank on the 14 August 2013. Officials say it is "highly unlikely" she will return to active service, but the final decision will be made only after the boat is re-floated and inspected.
Shishumar-class	Attack submarine	INS Shishumar (S44) INS Shankush (S45) INS Shalki (S46) INS Shankul (S47)	Germany	

(**Source:** Wikipedia)

Chart 13: Aircraft Carriers

Class	Type	Ships	Origin	Note
Centaur-class	Aircraft carrier	INS Viraat (R22)	United Kingdom	STOVL carrier.
Modified Kiev-class	Aircraft carrier	INS Vikramaditya (R33)	Russia	STOBAR carrier.

Chart 14: Amphibious Warfare Ships, Landing Ships

In addition, the Indian Navy maintains 6 landing craft (L-34 to L-39) that operate from and in conjunction with these vessels below. They serve to transport troops and equipment from ship to shore during an amphibious operation.

Class	Type	Ships	Origin	Dis-place-ment	Note
Aus-tin-class	Amphibi-ous trans-port dock (LPD)	INS Jalashwa (L41)	United States	16,590 tonnes	Under terms of sale, Jalashwa cannot be used during a war or offensive opera-tion, unless such action is granted by the United States Pentagon.
Shar-dul-class	Landing ship tank (LST)	INS Shardul (L16) INS Kesari (L15) INS Airavat (L24)	India	5,600 tonnes	
Magar-class	Landing ship tank (LST)	INS Magar (L20) INS Gharial (L23)	India	5,655 tonnes	
Kumb-hir-class	Landing ship tank (LST)	INS Cheetah (L18) INS Mahish (L19) INS Guldar (L21) INS Kumbhir (L22)	Poland	1,100 tonnes	

Chart 15: Destroyers and Frigates

Class	Type	Ships	Ori-gin	Note
Kolka-ta-class	Stealth Guided missile destroyer	INS Kolkata	India	Currently undergoing sea trials. Expected to be com-missioned by early 2014.

Class	Type	Ships	Origin	Note
Delhi-class	Guided missile destroyer	INS Delhi (D61) INS Mysore (D60) INS Mumbai (D62)	India	
Rajput-class	Guided missile destroyer	INS Rajput (D51) INS Rana (D52) INS Ranjit (D53) INS Ranvir (D54) INS Ranvijay (D55)	Soviet Union India	Build in Soviet Union. Indian design modifications to the Soviet Kashin class destroyers design.
Shivalik-class	Multi-role stealth frigate	INS Shivalik (F47) INS Satpura (F48) INS Sahyadri (F49)	India	
Talwar-class	Multi-role stealth frigate	INS Talwar (F40) INS Trishul (F43) INS Tabar (F44) INS Teg (F45) INS Tarkash (F50) INS Trikand (F51)	Russia	
Brahmaputra-class	Guided missile frigate	INS Brahmaputra (F31) INS Betwa (F39) INS Beas (F37)	India	
Godavari - class	Guided missile frigate	INS Godavari (F20) INS Ganga (F22) INS Gomati (F21)	India	

Chart 16: Corvettes

Class	Type	Ships	Origin	Note
Kamorta-class	Stealth ASW Corvette	INS Kamorta	India	Currently undergoing sea trials. Expected to be commissioned by early 2014.
Kora-class	Corvette	INS Kora (P61) INS Kirch (P62) INS Kulish (P63) INS Karmuk (P64)	India	
Khukri - class	Corvette	INS Khukri (P49) INS Kuthar (P46) INS Kirpan (P44) INS Khanjar (P47)	India	

Class	Type	Ships	Origin	Note
Veer-class	Corvette (light)	INS Veer (K40) INS Nirbhik (K41) INS Nipat (K42) INS Nishank (K43) INS Nirghat (K44) INS Vibhuti (K45) INS Vipul (K46) INS Vinash (K47) INS Vidyut (K48) INS Nashak (K83) INS Prabal (K92) INS Pralaya (K91)	India Soviet Union	Customized Indian variant of the Soviet Tarantul class.
Abhay - class	Corvette (light	INS Abhay (P33) INS Ajay (P34) INS Akshay (P35) INS Agray (P36)	India Soviet Union	Customized Indian variants of the Soviet Pauk class corvettes.

(**Source:** Wikipedia)

Chart 17: Mine Countermeasure Vessels

Class	Type	Ships	Origin	Note
Pondicherry - class	Minesweeper	INS Alleppey (M65) INS Karwar (M67) INS Cannanore (M68) INS Cuddalore (M69) INS Kakinanda (M70) INS Kozhikode (M71) INS Konkan (M72)	Soviet Union	

(**Source:** Wikipedia)

Chart 18: Miscellaneous

Class	Type	Ships	Origin	Note
Ambika-class	High sulphur diesel oiler	INS Ambika		Not listed on official Indian Navy website.
	Fuel carrier (barge)	INS Poshak	India	Not listed on official Indian Navy website.
Modest-Class	Fuel carrier (barge)	INS Purak INS Puran		Not listed on official Indian Navy website.
Hooghly-Class	Fuel carrier (barge)	INS		Not listed on official Indian Navy website.

Class	Type	Ships	Origin	Note
Vipul - Class	Water carrier (barge)	INS Pamba INS Pulakesin-1 INS Ambuda		Not listed on official Indian Navy website.
GSL - class	Small ferryboat	INS Manohar INS Modak INS Mangal INS Madhur INS Manorama INS Manjula		Not listed on official Indian Navy website.
Manoram - class	Small ferryboat	INS Manoram INSVihar		Not listed on official Indian Navy website.
Shalimar - class	Small ferryboat	INS		Not listed on official Indian Navy website.

(**Source:** Wikipedia)

India's Ten latest Defence Procurement

The Ministry of Defence is reportedly planning to double its arms procurement and spend over $20 billion (over Rs 120,000 crore), more than twice the amount spent in the past 10 years on an annual basis. On the table are major naval acquisition programmes, including buying six submarines for about $2.3 billion and $3 billion worth modernization of India's artillery corps.

Companies are, therefore, eyeing huge opportunities in the defence sector, also on the back of the India-US nuclear deal. For instance, US aerospace major Boeing alone sees a $20-billion opportunity in India's defence sector over the next decade. It is bidding for defence orders worth $15-$20 billion for F/A-18 Super Hornet combat jets, P8I maritime surveillance aircraft and Apache combat helicopters.

According to sources, India has an ageing fighter fleet, mostly a combination of Jaguars, Russian-made MiGs and French Mirage aircraft, and some are up for replacement. India had also ordered new MKI fighters from Russia. A Defence News report suggests that India will increase the number of Medium Multi-Role Combat Aircraft (MMRCA) it plans to buy to 200, opening the door for more than one supplier.[1]

1) F/A-18 Super Hornet combat jets

The Boeing F/A-18E/F Super Hornet is a supersonic carrier-capable fighter/attack aircraft. The Super Hornet, which is a larger and more advanced variant of the F/A-18C/D Hornet, was first ordered by the US Navy in 1992. It entered service with the US Navy in 1999. An early version was marketed by McDonnell Douglas as Hornet2000 in the 1980s. The Super Hornet is about 20 per cent larger, 7000 lb (3000 kg) heavier empty, and 15,000 lb (6800 kg) heavier at maximum weight than the original Hornet. It carries 33 per cent more internal fuel, increasing mission range by 41 per cent and endurance by 50 per cent over the 'Legacy'.

2) P8I maritime surveillance aircraft

The Boeing P8I maritime patrol aircraft, which the Indian Navy is on the verge of acquiring, will give it a marked edge in the Indian Ocean region and one that is comparable to its US counterpart. The P8I, a customized version for the Indian Navy, is based on the hugely successful Boeing-737 commercial airliner. The Navy had in November 2006 expressed an interest in the aircraft as a replacement for its existing fleet of Il-38 aircraft that are nearing the end of their service life.

3) Apache combat helicopters

The AH-64D Apache helicopter is an advanced, versatile, survivable, deployable and maintainable multi-role combat helicopter. The new Apache helicopter integrates digital avionics and weapons, and the powerful T700-GE-701C engine. The

1. The Economic Times, 'India's Ten Latest Defence Procurement Programmes', (November 2008) http://economictimes.indiatimes.com/indias-10-latest-defence-procurement-programmes/slideshow/3694983.cms (Accessed in August 2012)

AH-64D Apache helicopter's predecessor is the battle-proven AH-64A Apache helicopter. However, the new Apache helicopter is built for the digital battlefield of the future.

4) Mig-29K (Fulcrum-D) fighters

The government is also likely to buy 30 more carrier borne Mig-29K (Fulcrum-D) fighters for the Indian Navy, according to news reports. Russians have demanded a price escalation of $2 billion, almost double the original contract cost of $2.5 billion for refurbishing the 45,000-tonne carrier, including carrying out its elaborate sea trials in Russian waters, prior to its delivery by 2012. Under the 2004 contract for the acquisition of Admiral Gorshkov aircraft carrier, India is to receive 12 single-seater MiG-29K and 4 units of two-seater MiG-29KUB by next year, with an option of ordering additional 30 fighters by 2015.

5) Ka-31 helicopters, Il-38D aircraft

Besides Mig-29K fighters, Indian Navy is also procuring other advanced aircraft to support fleet operations. These include Ka-31 airborne early warning helicopters for the carriers, and land-based Il-38D maritime patrol aircraft.

6) Spyder missile

India has recently signed an agreement with Israel to acquire 18 Spyder surface to air missiles to protect high-value assets of the Indian Air Force. The plans to acquire the Spyder had been announced in 2006 but were on hold due to allegations of corruption over the Israeli Barak missiles deal for the Indian Navy signed four years ago. But as neither the IAF nor the Navy and Army have adequate missile defence protection, the government has been under pressure to do the needful for several years. Spyder is a static low level, quick reaction missile (LLQRM) to neutralize hostile targets up to 15 km away, and at heights between 20 to 9000 meters

7) Akash surface to air missile

The Indian Air Force is also in the process of acquiring the indigenous Akash surface to air missile which has a little longer effective range of 25 km as part of a layered approach to defend its assets. Both the Spyder and Akash are all weather missiles, 24 x 7 and 360 degrees with autonomous management and advanced Electronic Counter Measures (ECCM) capability. It can be launched within five seconds, and once the commander has pressed the button, the process to seek and engage an aggressive aircraft or missile is automatic.

8) Hawk Mk-132 advanced jet trainer

In a step with major implications for pilot training, the Indian Air Force recently got its first indigenously built Hawk Mk-132 advanced jet trainer (AJT), manufactured at the state-owned Hindustan Aeronautics Ltd (HAL). Powered by a single Rolls-Royce Adour Mk 871 turbofan engine, the aircraft is the first of 42 Hawk aircraft being built under licence by HAL in India, and is the 15th Hawk AJT handed over to the IAF. The engine is a newer version of the Adour Mk 811 that HAL already builds for the IAF Jaguar strike aircraft. HAL is building 49 of these engines, but later, the same engine will also be fitted on the six Hercules C 130Js that IAF is acquiring from the US arms major, Lockheed Martin. Each of these special role aircraft will be fitted with four engines, so the IAF requirement could be around 30 additional engines for them including spares.

9) Multi Role Combat Aircraft

IAF is also likely to start getting delivery of its 126 Multi Role Combat Aircraft (MRCAs) from 2012 onwards. According to reports, six contenders were due to submit their response to the Request for Proposal (RfPs) or tenders by March and ministry of defence sources had indicated that it should not take them more than a year-and-a-half to examine and clear the IAF recommendations in making the choice and placing the order. Indications are that eventually, with indigenous production, the number of MRCAs could go up to 200 or more.

10) Fifth Generation Fighter Aircraft

The Fifth Generation Fighter Aircraft (FGFA) for the Indian Air Force is likely to be inducted in 2016. India and Russia had agreed to co-develop the FGFA and an agreement was signed in this regard some time back when defence minister A K Antony had visited Moscow in October last year.

Bibliography

- Annual Reports of Ministry of Defence (MoD)
- Defence Service Estimate Report, Government of India (1950-2013)
- Ministry of Defence Annual Reports, Government of India (1950-2013)
- Subhramanyam, K. 'Kargil Review Committee Report, July 1999
- Jawaharlal Nehru's Speeches, Vol.5, 1963-64 (New Delhi: Publications Division, 1968), p.187.
- Athawale. S. Sanhita (2004), "Defence Services", New Delhi, Anmol Publications Pvt. Ltd.
- Awasthi Soumya, (2014) 'Trends In India's Defence Budget 1950-Till date', India's National Security in the 21st Century, ed., New Delhi, Pentagon Press
- Ghosh Kumar Amiya (2006), "Defence Budgeting and Planning in India: The Way Forward", New Delhi, Knowledge World
- Global Defence "Offset Review", (2014)
- 'Horns of a Dilemma: Purchase or Produce?', "Defence Production in India", New Delhi
- George K. Tanham,(1992) 'Indian Strategic Thought: An Interpretive Essay', RAND
- Joshi Praveen (2005) 'India's Defence Expenditure: Historical Perspective', Emerging India: Security and Foreign Policy Perspectives, Ed. New Delhi, Institute

for Defence Studies and Analysis and Promilla & Co. Publishers

- Kavic. Lorne (1967) "India's Quest for Security: Defence Policies, 1947-1965", Berkeley and Los Angeles, University of California Press.
- Karnad Bharat, (2005) 'India's Future Plans and Defence Requirements', "Emerging India: Security and Foreign Policy Perspectives" ed., New Delhi, Institute for Defence Studies and Analysis and Promilla & Co., Publishers
- Kennedy Gavin,(1975) 'The Economics of Defence', Faber and Faber, London
- Lakshmi Y, (1988) Trends in India's Defence Expenditure, New Delhi ABC Publication House.
- Lakshmi Y, (May 1986), 'Defence Expenditure- An Asset or a Burden? Strategic Analysis, New Delhi, Institute for Defence Studies and Analysis.
- Mathews Ron, (1989) Defence Production in India, New Delhi, ABC Publication House.
- Paranjpe Shrikant, (1999) 'A Framework for Analysis of India's Security Expenditures', "Perspectives on India's Defence and Arms Control" ed., University of Mumbai, Department of Civics and Politics.
- Paranjpe Shrikant, (1993) Mondes En Developpement-TOME21, 'Beyond the Defence and Development: A Framework for Analysis of Indian Expenditure'
- Srinivas V.N, (2008) "Budgeting for Indian Defence: Issues of Contemporary Relevance", New Delhi, K.W Publishers
- Singh Jasjit, (2005) 'Aerospace Challenges for India' "Emerging India: Security and Foreign Policy Perspectives" ed., New Delhi, Institute for Defence Studies and Analysis and Promilla & Co., Publishers.
- Stewart Frances, (2001) 'Development and Security', Taylor& Francis

- Singh Jasjit, (2001), "India's Defence Spending: Assessing Future Needs", Institute for Defence Studies and Analysis and Knowledge World, New Delhi
- Singh Jasjit (1999) 'Trends in Defence Expenditure', ed. Asian Strategic Review 1998-99 (New Delhi: Institute for Defence Studies and Analysis.
- Thomas G.C Raju, (1980) 'The Armed Services and the India Defence Budget', Asian Survey, Vol. XX no. 3, March 1980
- Acquisition community connection, "DoD Template for Application of TLCSM and PBL In the Weapon System Life Cycle", https://acc.dau.mil/CommunityBrowser.aspx (Accessed in January 2014)
- Ajit Doval, "India's Internal and External Security: Areas that call for greater national attention",(Sep2012) http://ajitdoval.blogspot.in/2012/09/indias-internal-and-external-security.html (Accessed in October 2012)
- Ajit Doval, "India's Defence Production and Research – Need for Transformational up-gradation", (Feb2012) http://www.vifindia.org/article/2012/february/06/India-s-Defence-Production-and-Research-Need-for-Transformational-up-gradation. (Accessed in Feb2012)
- Behera Laxman, "An American Solution to India's Defence Acquisition Problem?"(Oct 2010) http://idsa.in/idsacomments/AnAmericanSolutiontoIndiasDefenceAcquisitionProblem_lkbehera_081010, (Accessed in October 2013)
- Behera Kumar, Laxman ' India's Defence Budget 2012-13 ', (June, 2012)
  http://www.defencereviewasia.com/articles/169/India-s-Defence-Budget-2012-13 (Accessed in August 2012)
- Bikramdeep Singh, "Time for Adopting a Life Cycle Approach to Defence Acquisitions" (December 2013) http://www.claws.in/Time-for-Adopting-a-Life-Cycle-

Approach-to-Defence-Acquisitions-Bikramdeep-Singh.html (Accessed in December 2013)

- Bikramdeep Singh, "Time for Adopting a Life Cycle Approach to Defence Acquisitions", (Jan 2014) Indian Defence Review, http://www.indiandefencereview.com/spotlights/time-for-adopting-a-life-cycle-approach-to-defence-acquisitions/ (Accessed in January 2014)
- Chenok Dan, "Eight Action to Improves Defence Acquisition" (December 2013) Federal Times, http://www.federaltimes.com/article/20131217/ACQ02/312170013/Eight-actions-improve-defense-acquisition (Accessed in December 2013)
- Confederation of Indian Industry, Defence Division http://www.ciidefence.com/defenceindustry.asp?id=1 (Accessed in January 2014)
- Defence Advanced Research Project Agency (DARPA), Home page, http://www.darpa.mil/default.aspx (Accessed in February 2014)
- Flight Global, "List of latest weapons and Equipments" (Set 2013) http://www.flightglobal.com/news/military/ (Accessed in November 2013)
- G Servants, 'VII Pay Commission: First CPC to Third CPC Pay Scales', (Feb 2013) http://www.gservants.com/2013/02/11/vii-pay-commission-first-cpc-to-third-cpc-pay-scales/, (Accessed in February 2013)
- Hardy James, "India's Defence Procurement Bungles", (October 2013) The Diplomat, http://thediplomat.com/2013/10/indias-defense-procurement-bungles/?allpages=yes (Accessed in October 2013)
- Masters, Jonathan, 'Defence Spending and Deficit Debate', (Nov 2011) Council on Foreign Relations, http://www.cfr.org/defense-budget/defense-spending-deficit-debate/p26442 (Accessed in January 2013)

- Mohan C. Raja, (2004) 'India's "look-west" policy', http://www.hindu.com/2004/06/17/stories/2004061700831000.htm (Accessed on November 2013)
- Nation Master 'India Economy Stats', , http://www.nationmaster.com/country-info/profiles/India/Economy (Accessed in January 2014)
- Press Information Bureau, Government of India, 'Salient Features of Defence Procurement Procedure- 2013' http://pib.nic.in/newsite/erelease.aspx?relid=96361 (Accessed in July 2013)
- Revi A.P, "Revolution in military logistics", Indian Defence Review, (Feb 2008)http://www.indiandefencereview.com/spotlights/revolution-in-military-logistics/ (Accessed in November 2013)
- Stockholm International Peace Research Institute. "Monitoring Military Expenditures", http://www.sipri.org/research/armaments/milex/measuring-military-expenditures (Accessed in March 2013)
- Singh Navdeep, 'IAS Officers to get the pay scale of Major General in 14 years of service', (April 2008) , http://www.indianmilitary.info/2008/04/ias-officers-to-get-payscale-of-major.html (Accessed in November 2012)
- Srinath, The Transition State, "In Pragati: Understanding India's Defence Spending",(Sep 2013) http://catalyst.nationalinterest.in/2013/09/23/pragati-infographic-india-defence-spending/ (Accessed in November 2013)
- The Economist, "India as a great power Know your own strength" (March 2013) http://www.economist.com/news/briefing/21574458-india-poised-become-one-four-largest-military-powers-world-end. (Accessed in April 2013)
- The Economic Times, 'India's Ten Latest Defence Procurement Programmes', (November 2008) http://economictimes.indiatimes.com/indias-10-latest-defence-

procurement-programmes/slideshow/3694983.cms (Accessed in August 2012)

- Value of Dissent, "Public Expenditure and Defence Budgeting in India",(May 2012) http://valueofdissent.files.wordpress.com/2012/05/ministry-of-defence-india.jpg (Accessed on March 2013)

Index

Symbols

A

B

C

D

E

F

J

K

L

M

N

R

S